Decolonizing Preaching

LLOYD JOHN OGILVIE INSTITUTE
OF PREACHING SERIES

SERIES EDITORS:

Clayton J. Schmit
Mark Labberton

The vision of the Lloyd John Ogilvie Institute of Preaching is to proclaim Jesus Christ and to catalyze a movement of empowered, wise preachers who seek justice, love mercy, and walk humbly with God, leading others to join in God's mission in the world. The books in this series are selected to contribute to the development of such wise and humble preachers. The authors represent both scholars of preaching as well as pastors and preachers whose experiences and insights can contribute to passionate and excellent preaching.

CURRENT VOLUMES IN THIS SERIES:

The Eloquence of Grace: Joseph Sittler and the Preaching Life edited by James M. Childs Jr. and Richard Lischer

The Preacher as Liturgical Artist: Metaphor, Identity, and the Vicarious Humanity of Christ by Trygve David Johnson

Ordinary Preacher, Extraordinary Gospel: A Daily Guide for Wise, Empowered Preachers by Chris Neufeld-Erdman

Blessed and Beautiful: Multiethnic Churches and the Preaching That Sustains Them by Lisa Washington Lamb

FORTHCOMING VOLUMES IN THIS SERIES:

Youthful Preaching: Strengthening the Relationship Between Youth, Adults, and Preaching by Richard W. Voelz

Decolonizing Preaching

The Pulpit as Postcolonial Space

Sarah Travis

CASCADE *Books* · Eugene, Oregon

DECOLONIZING PREACHING
The Pulpit as Postcolonial Space

Lloyd John Ogilvie Institute of Preaching Series 6

Cascade Books
An Imprint of Wipf and Stock Publishers
199 W. 8th Ave., Suite 3
Eugene, OR 97401

www.wipfandstock.com

ISBN 13: 978-1-62564-528-9

Cataloguing-in-Publication data:

Travis, Sarah.

    Decolonizing preaching : the pulpit as postcolonial space / Sarah Travis.

    x + 152 pp. ; 23 cm. Includes bibliographical references.

    Lloyd John Ogilvie Institute of Preaching Series 6

    ISBN 13: 978-1-62564-528-9

    1. Preaching. 2. Postcolonialism. 3. Trinity. I. Title. II. Series.

BV4211.2 T72 2014

Manufactured in the U.S.A.

For Ben and Ella, with hope that your world will be different.

Contents

Acknowledgments

THIS PROJECT OWES ITS existence to a great cloud of witnesses who have supported and encouraged me. I am grateful to the faculty, staff, and students of Knox College, University of Toronto for their companionship. Especially Dr. Dorcas Gordon, for her inspiring leadership and unflagging enthusiasm. Thanks also to Dr. David Jacobsen for his faith in this project, and relentless commitment to the theological imperative of preaching. I have had the privilege to learn with and from many other homileticians at the Toronto School of Theology, including Paul Scott Wilson, Sarah Freeman, Sam Persons Parkes, and Kyongkuk Han. Although any errors in this book are my own, Lianne Biggar provided wonderful technical support to the development of this manuscript.

My interest in the ongoing effects of colonialism/imperialism has come about partly because of my relationship with the Christians of the Vindhya Satpura region of India. I am continually humbled by the faithfulness of those communities, and in awe of their great capacity for hospitality. As always, I am filled with admiration for Dr. Pauline Brown and Dr. Wilma Welsh who introduced me to a whole other world. Closer to home, I have been blessed to share in the life of Trafalgar Presbyterian Church, Oakville. Thanks to Rev. Kristine O'Brien, Rev. Karen Pozios, and their families for creating spaces for rest, dialogue, and recreation.

Most of all, thank you to my husband, Paul Miller. You have been chief cheerleader, sounding board, proofreader, and friend. What a wonderful thing it is to share life with you and our children. This particular project began with great loss, the death of our son Sam in 2007. Yet we have discovered that new life grows even when we least expect it. Indeed, the best is yet to come.

Introduction

THIS BOOK IS A few centuries too late. Colonialism, imperialism, and the omnipresence of empire have shaped and stretched the Christian church since its inception. Preaching has always occurred in the midst of empire, in a world where peoples and nations have been traded like pawns—some crowned royalty, and others pushed right off the game board. This book is too late because the damage has already been done. Colonialism and similar processes have divided and conquered human relationships, often unchallenged by those of us who preach the good news of God's kingdom. This book is too late because we have entered a postcolonial era. The age of colonialism is over. Or is it? As with other *posts*, the term "postcolonial" must be handled with care. Postcolonial does not necessarily indicate the end of colonialism, as if all its messy complications and broken pieces have been swept up neatly and tidied away. Nor does it imply that we have entered a time after colonialism. Instead, the term "postcolonial" recognizes that we exist in a state of continuity and discontinuity with colonial/imperial projects. That is, we are still living the consequences of colonial history and encountering colonialism in contemporary guises.

Today, we continue to preach in the midst of empire, even as the face of empire continues to morph and change. This book, then, is not too late after all. It is time for those of us who preach to consider colonial realities and the impact of those realities upon the communities we serve. It is time for those of us who preach to reimagine our task as one that contributes to a process of repairing, reconciling, and renewing a global community that has been torn and bruised by the ongoing imperial tug of war. It is also time to celebrate what God has done and is doing to bring good out of a troubled human history.

Preaching is a theological act that names, out loud, the world as it is and as it may become. In what sense do we, as preachers in the United States and Canada, live in a context of continuity and discontinuity with colonialism/imperialism? While this question will be explored throughout this book, it is helpful to clarify the meaning of these terms. Colonialism and imperialism share ideological roots. While acknowledging that there are differences between these terms, I have chosen here to highlight their interconnectedness and common effects by denoting them as a single term: *colonialism/imperialism.*

Colonialism refers to the settlement and/or exploitation of a territory by foreign agents. Historically, powerful nations have identified other regions that are rich in natural and human resources. Through various degrees of force, the powerful nations have implanted settlers, governance and military leaders in other lands. The British Empire, for example, was so keen to control vast stretches of the world's surface that by the early twentieth century, approximately one-fifth of the world's population, and one-quarter of the world's land mass were under the control of the United Kingdom. The modern era, especially the industrial revolution, increased the need for cheap labor and copious material resources. Colonialism enabled the exploration and exploitation of regions rich in material and human resources. Yet colonialism precedes the modern era. Ancient empires established a practice that was copied and expanded by later empires.

Imperialism is the ideology from which colonialism arises. This ideology justifies and enables foreign control and exploitation of other peoples. Empires came to exist because particular nations or groups determined that they had a right or responsibility to attain the resources of others and to control foreign populations. Many of the great international conflicts of the modern era can be attributed at least in part to competition among imperial powers seeking to control the regions with the most valuable resources.

Colonialism/imperialism generally resulted in the occupation of distant lands and varying degrees of military dominance. It also resulted in unequal relationships of power and knowledge across national and cultural boundaries in a variety of historical and contemporary settings. The colonizers—those who had the financial means, military might, and perceived warrant to control other people—achieved tremendous power in the world. In many historical instances colonizers gained not only physical control over other populations but also claimed the right of cultural superiority. The colonizer then was at the center of a system that pushed the colonized to the margins. Colonialism/imperialism, and related systems such as neocolonialism and globalization, have contributed to the formation of identity in the modern era. With colonialism came the mixing of populations, global travel, and frequently the relocation and settlement of large populations. Slavery, for example, was an extreme act that stemmed from the need of empires to staff their colonial projects: the cultivation of crops such as sugar, cotton, and tobacco required vast human resources. In some locations settlement was achieved with less violence, at least for white Christian populations. For example, the British immigrants arriving in the United States and Canada often came willingly, albeit in order to escape oppression and poverty in their homeland. Once established in the new land, however, recent white settlers participated in the project of extracting and controlling the rich resources at hand.

Relationships among colonizers and colonized persons have been complex and multifaceted. While it is tempting to view colonial relationships as straightforward oppressor-colonizer versus oppressed-colonized, history has been much more complicated. Colonized persons retain some degree of power, and the power of colonizers is less than absolute. Depending on the nature of the colony, the relationship among the colonizers and colonized persons might be cordial (the relationship of English settlers in Canada with the British crown) or fraught (as it was for some settlers in the United States). There is always a degree of ambiguity in colonial relationships.

Much of this business of colonialism/imperialism seems to be mere history. Yet the contemporary world exists as it does because of colonial/imperial history. As formerly colonized nations have gained independence, global relations have not automatically equalized. Unequal relationships remain between those who are or have been world powers and those who are or have been at the receiving end of colonial intrusion. This book is concerned with the way that discourses of power continue, just as colonialism/imperialism continues today, albeit in different guises. Colonizing discourse refers to the use of language and symbol that seeks to maintain an impenetrable boundary between center and margins. This destructive discourse sneaks into our relationships both globally and locally. Colonizing discourse has serious consequences for the Christian church and the whole human community, and special implications for the practice of preaching.

At the heart of this book is a critique of the colonizing discourse that continues to negatively influence personal and communal relationships.

My critique arises in part from a postcolonial perspective. The term "post-colonial" resists simple definition, and its meaning is multifaceted and often disputed. I use the term "postcolonial" to represent the ongoing reality of those whose social histories have been shaped and continue to be shaped culturally, psychologically, and economically by the reality of colonialism/imperialism and the concomitant interplay of power related to gender, race, and class. The past stubbornly refuses to stay in the past, and colonizing discourse interrupts many of our contemporary conversations. Despite the prevalence of the term "postcolonial," colonial legacies persist in North America. Not only have historical colonial projects influenced the populations of Canada and the United States, but the power of empires still looms large in cultural, economic, and even theological spheres. Empire is not limited to national interests but includes both national and international systems that wield control over global populations. Media, consumer culture, world financial systems, military alliances—each represents concrete or ideological aspects of contemporary empire. Empire attempts to dictate and maintain a particular world order and systems that are frequently harmful to the majority of the world's population.

A postcolonial perspective denotes a desire to recognize and interrupt colonizing discourses and to uncover embedded colonial/imperial assumptions that guide daily life. Postcolonial theory has been brought to bear on many academic disciplines, including biblical and theological studies, and has much to contribute to the theory and practice of preaching. The theory and practice of preaching are not immune to colonizing discourse. A significant task of preachers living in a contemporary, hybridized culture is to consider whether and how preaching must be decolonized. A postcolonial perspective on preaching investigates both homiletic theory and practice for colonizing discourse and embedded colonial/imperial assumptions. It identifies how preaching may potentially participate in oppression and dehumanization or, alternatively, participate in transforming human community. Such a perspective assumes that preaching occurs in contexts impacted by colonialism/imperialism, that both preachers and listeners occupy a variety of postcolonial positions and bear varying colonial/imperial memories and experiences. This is not to say that most preachers use power inappropriately or intentionally subordinate listeners. Rather, it is to assume that all of us—preachers and listeners—exist in a time and place in which colonialism echoes and reverberates. Contemporary preaching occurs in postmodern, globalized, and diverse settings. Preaching also occurs in the midst of empire. Preaching is relational; it shapes a particular community of faith and belongs to a much broader, global ecclesial discourse. Preaching is a task that is central to the development of Christian identity and ethics. Thus, it is essential for preachers to consider empire as one of many conditions that affect the church and the world beyond.

Colonizing discourse is destructive to human relationships. It runs contrary to a vision for human community that is rooted in the mission of the Triune God. In order to situate the problem of decolonizing preaching within a solid theological framework, I partner postcolonial theory with a distinct, Trinitarian theological vision for human community. Social Trinitarian theologies provide a discourse that contradicts colonizing discourse: insofar as Christians seek to reconstruct faith communities in the image of the Trinity, we will overcome some of the more destructive legacies of colonialism/imperialism.

Preaching is a means of decolonizing relationships within the church and beyond the church. To preach the good news of God's kingdom is to speak a resounding "no" to discourses that seek to dominate, separate, and homogenize others. When our preaching offers an alternative discourse rooted in God's own nature, we commit an act of treason against the empires of this world by proclaiming that God alone is the source and sustainer of life. Preachers and listeners occupy an in-between space: between past and present, between center and margins, between the powerful and powerless, between the kingdom of God and the kingdoms of this world. It is the task of this book to begin to imagine this in-between space as a place of re-creation, reconciliation, and reorientation of power. This project is really about redemption, examining the consequences of colonialism/imperialism and asking what God can do with it and asking what God can do with it. God's work in the world via the Trinity has prepared us for such a time as this. The story of God-with-us is itself a story that seeks to break down boundaries and challenge the empires of this world.

Who should read this book?

Decolonizing preaching is a necessary task for those of us who recognize that empire is still a force with which to be reckoned. My hope is that this book will benefit scholars and teachers of preaching, practitioners, and students. It is directed at middle-class North Americans whose ethnic and cultural backgrounds are of European origin, many of whom serve culturally diverse congregations. It especially concerns citizens of nations that loom large on the world stage and operate within capitalist economic systems. Within these pages there is food for thought for those concerned about the postmodern ethos, those wrestling with issues of power inequality, and those looking for a manageable introduction to postcolonial thought. Preachers engage in a weekly homiletic conversation with a mix of both colonized and colonizing persons. We gather in churches that have been associated with colonial missions. We are representatives and servants of a church that has borne a tremendous degree of social and spiritual power yet finds itself simultaneously unsure of its location in the contemporary social hierarchy. Any preacher who has wrestled with these issues will find a space for reflection in the pages of this book.

Some might wonder why a Western woman of relative privilege should undertake this project. I critique colonizing discourse as a white female Canadian Presbyterian, despite Rebecca Todd Peter's observation that "the examination of a postcolonial perspective on the Church may, at first glance, seem an imperialistic impossibility for a white, affluent, Protestant woman from [the United States]."[1] I consider myself to live at the crossroads of empire as a citizen of a nation and a minister of a church, both of which have been implicated in colonialism/imperialism. My husband works for one of the original Canadian railway companies that charged ahead with westward expansion in the earliest days of Canada's nationhood at great cost to Canada's aboriginal peoples and countless Asian immigrants who were employed in the dangerous task of railway building. Thus, most of our household income stems from organizations that have been complicit in colonial/imperial projects.

The consequences of empire have far-reaching tentacles: both metropolis and colony have been and continue to be negatively affected by the colonial/imperial process, resulting in a diminishment of human life and spirituality. The task of decolonizing the mind is as essential to the colonizer as it is to the colonized.[2] I tread these postcolonial pathways with care, recognizing that some will wonder at my audacity to speak against a system from which I benefit. My hope is to enter into conversation with others who will critique and enlarge the perspective offered here. Postcolonial theory desires to complexify rather than simplify human relationships. A postcolonial homiletic cannot be constructed by one voice alone but will be built

1. Peters, "Decolonizing our Minds," 99.
2. Ibid.

upon the experiences of many. This project is only a beginning. Despite my desire to problematize binary oppositions, they are at times difficult to avoid if I am to salvage clarity. While this book is focused on preaching and ecclesial practice, there are benefits beyond the body of Christ, including public theology, inter-faith dialogue, and responses to global need and poverty. All of these issues find their way into preaching. For the sake of listeners, the church, and the world beyond the church, it is time to take seriously the homiletical implications of colonizing discourse.

Outline

Part I examines the colonial/imperial setting of the United States and Canada in order to develop an understanding of the postcolonial context of preaching today. Perhaps the most heart-wrenching task of decolonizing preaching is coming to terms with global and ecclesial history. There are countless examples of "historical resistance, complicity and bystander practices of Christians in relation to global violence."[3] Chapter 1 traces the history of modern colonialism/imperialism, paying special attention to the occasions in which colonial history overlaps with the mission of the Christian church. It is impossible to consider Western colonialism/imperialism outside of its position within Christendom. This chapter focuses on the manner in which the United States and Canada have been implicated in colonial/imperial projects. What is the legacy of colonialism/imperialism for contemporary life? Where is colonizing discourse still whispered aloud or acted out in symbolic ways? In order to root out colonizing discourse, one must be able to identify it. I outline its key characteristics in terms of domination, separation, homogenization, and fixedness.

Once the history and legacy of colonialism/imperialism are named and colonizing discourse is defined, it is time to explore the implications for preaching. Chapter 2 begins by situating the current context of preaching in the postcolonial era. Preaching both contributes to and is shaped by the worldview, ethics, and identity of preacher and listeners. How will a postcolonial perspective on preaching interact with ethics and identity? What are the consequences for the church and the world beyond the church? I go on to identify spaces within the development and delivery of sermons that are most vulnerable to colonizing discourse, and I name the tasks that will need to be accomplished if we are to begin decolonizing preaching.

3. Sharp, *Misunderstanding Stories*, 3–4.

Part II provides an ideological and theological framework for postcolonial preaching. Chapter 3 offers a theological critique of colonizing discourse that is rooted in the Triune God. Social Trinitarian formulations of God's nature and identity postulate an equal relationship among Creator, Son, and Holy Spirit that is characterized by mutual self-giving, self-differentiation, and openness. These characteristics are deeply at odds with the characteristics of colonizing discourse. The nature of the Trinity effectively deconstructs the foundations of colonizing discourse and casts a vision of human relationship that transcends the limits imposed by empire. The Trinity, then, provides a theological foundation and practical instruction for the goal of decolonizing preaching. Chapter 4 traces the development of postcolonial theory, introduces some key terminology, and highlights strategies for approaching colonizing discourse.

Equipped with theological, theoretical, and practical strategies for critiquing colonizing discourse, it is time to develop a toolbox for preaching that can effectively recognize colonizing discourse and speak an alternative discourse.

Part III incorporates postcolonial theory and Social Trinitarian theology in order to develop an accessible and useful approach for preachers desiring to respond to colonialism/imperialism in their sermons. Chapter 5 invites preachers to foster a postcolonial imagination that considers the manner in which preachers use knowledge, represent others, and develop an awareness of their own power relative to their listeners. An important aspect of such an imaginative stance is the ability to recognize and name colonizing discourse as it occurs in the church, the pulpit, and the pew. Preachers are encouraged to locate an alternative discourse that can adequately respond to colonizing discourse as it is found within the church. This chapter outlines a number of concrete strategies that will enable preachers to speak a word that matters into a postcolonial context.

The weekly preaching event for most preachers begins with the Bible. Scripture is the source and norm for preaching, yet even the Bible is not immune from colonial/imperial forces. It was developed in a colonial era, has been implicated in colonial projects, and today it is preached in the midst of empire. Chapter 6 examines the Bible in its colonial/imperial context, from the manner in which texts have been used to justify colonial/imperial projects to the various responses to empire embedded in the text. A growing body of postcolonial biblical criticism literature is a useful conversation partner for preachers and leads to a user-friendly hermeneutic for weekly exegesis.

Finally, chapter 7 explores the possibilities of recreation, reconciliation, and hope that arise within the embrace of Creator, Son, and Spirit. The intersection of postcolonial theories and Trinitarian theologies creates a productive and constructive space in which transformation can occur as God breathes new life into relationships that have been destroyed or endangered.

PART I

The Omnipresence of Empire

CHAPTER 1

Coming to Terms with Empire

IN MARCH 2011, A severe earthquake and tsunami devastated parts of Japan. As the world responded with an outpouring of sympathy and generosity, a markedly different reaction arose in China. Some Chinese citizens viewed the devastation in Japan as an opportunity to celebrate the misery of their former occupiers. The Chinese people have not forgotten the atrocities committed against them by Japan during its occupation of China in the 1930s and 1940s, when at least twenty million Chinese were killed. In some Chinese schools today, children are shown documentary films designed to inspire a continuing hatred for the Japanese. As one Chinese parent blogged: "It is the responsibility of every Chinese father and mother to pass down this history to their children in addition to what they learn in school. . . . I have not forgotten and I will not forgive." This attitude was not shared by all, and as the Chinese were confronted with the images of Japan's suffering caused by the terrible natural disaster, some began to reconsider their initial response. Hatred turned to awe as they witnessed the courage and perseverance of the Japanese people.[1]

The shadow of Japanese imperial power persists decades after Japan's withdrawal from China. The Chinese are not alone in harboring negative feelings toward former colonizers. Other formerly colonized nations also bear strong feelings toward previous oppressors, although these emotions are frequently mixed and range from hatred to ambivalence to friendship. Colonial/imperial acts do not remain in the past but affect the present. Memories continue to impact relationships among those who have been victims, perpetrators, and observers of colonial/imperial acts long after

1. Schiller, "In China, Awe and Admiration for Japan."

occupation ends. Colonialism/imperialism in contemporary guise combines with distant memory to produce a continued context of empire.

Much of world history in the last centuries has been defined by colonialism/imperialism. The twentieth century was a time of heightened international conflict integrally related to empire, along with several significant examples of decolonization, and the rise of neocolonialism and globalization. Today, North American preachers find ourselves in a space that has been and continues to be shaped by colonialism/imperialism. Pews are filled by a faithful multiplicity: individuals with differing cultural, ethnic, and national identities. We have unprecedented access to information about global others. Our governments act on a global stage. As consumers, we are invited to partake of an international smorgasbord of goods and foods.

Some of those who gather for worship remember what it is to live under the domination of another group. Others continue to experience marginalization. Some are members of dominant groups and experience the privilege of living at the center of society. All of these realities are related to histories and legacies of colonialism/imperialism. All of these realities will affect the relationships among Christians and others. I believe that preaching is to some extent about relationship. Preaching nurtures Christian identity, Christian community, and the connections among Christians and others beyond the church. Yet colonialism/imperialism is also about relationship. It involves a careful structuring of relationships between groups and individuals in terms of power. In many ways, as we shall see, the relational structure of colonialism/imperialism is distinctly at odds with the relational imperatives of Christianity.

Empire brings to mind the ancient civilizations of Greece, Rome, Babylon, Persia. With the rise of global navigation, the ancient empires gave way to new empires that controlled vast stretches of the world's surface, perhaps most notably the British Empire. Today, the United States carries imperial weight and creates shifting alliances with other world powers resulting in global institutions that mimic empire. The reality of empire has been ubiquitous, ever present, forming the invisible foundation of daily life. Our world today has been so shaped by empire that it is impossible to untangle the imperial threads that have led us to this point in history. Empire can be considered

> a coming together of economic, cultural, political and military
> power in our world . . . constituted by a reality and a spirit of

lordless domination, created by humankind. An all-encompassing global reality serving, protecting and defending the interests of powerful corporations, nations, elites and privileged people, while exploiting creation, imperiously excludes, enslaves and even sacrifices humanity.[2]

This definition of empire is intensely biased against empire, and considers the dramatic human cost of colonial/imperial projects. As a whole, colonialism/imperialism has tended to benefit wealthy colonizing nations while denying the autonomy of colonized nations. The consequences of some imperial projects have been severe and inexcusable, including the sale and transport of human beings to support the economic goals of empires. The wealth of empires has been built on oppression and exploitation. In 2001, the United Nations "World Conference against Racism, Racial Discrimination, Xenophobia and Related Intolerance" affirmed that colonialism has caused suffering, and "must be condemned and its reoccurrence prevented." The report names the "lasting social and economic inequalities" that are a legacy of colonialism, and relates it to slavery, apartheid, and ongoing issues of racism throughout the world.[3]

Despite the human cost of colonial/imperial power, it is impossible to imagine our world today without the advances and possibilities that have come about because of colonialism/imperialism. Without colonies, the Romans might not have developed such intricate travel systems and roads. The countries of North America would not exist at all. Cultures and nations would lack diversity. Global trade would be limited. Would we travel as freely? Would our lives be enhanced by the knowledge of other languages and cultures? The Christian church would likely not have grown and spread as rapidly and thoroughly, and we would not enjoy the global partnerships of the worldwide communion of Jesus Christ. As drastic as the human cost has been in many situations, colonialism/imperialism has also had benefits for some colonized persons. From the present vantage point, it is unreasonable to condemn an entire economic and cultural system, just as it is unreasonable to celebrate such a system. The threads of colonialism/imperialism are tangled, and those of us who live in the twenty-first century have only a partial view of world history, which is so often only half a story. The point is not to stand in judgment of the past, but to cast a critical eye over the colonial and imperial systems as they exist in both past and present, and to

2. Boesak et al., *Dreaming a Different World*, 2.

3. United Nations Declaration, "World Conference Against Racism," 7.

reflect on those legacies that are barriers to positive human community in the here and now.

How Did We Get Here?

In order to consider the implications of preaching in the midst of empire, I begin by tracing the historical contours of the current context of churches in Canada and the United States. What is colonialism/imperialism, and how did it unfold in the European context during the last several hundred years? What has been the role of the Christian church with regard to modern colonial projects? What are the hallmarks of colonizing discourse, and how has this discourse been engaged in historical and contemporary contexts? A brief overview of modern colonial/imperial history will situate our present reality.

Since Christopher Columbus sailed the ocean blue in 1492, the power of Europe has moved outwards to the farthest reaches of the earth. A continually changing political landscape emerged as nations scrambled for control of the world's human and natural resources. The British Empire at various points in history claimed Canada, Australia, the United States (before it was the United States), Hong Kong, and India. The French had territory in what is now Canada, West Africa, and in the early twentieth century the French claimed one-tenth of the earth's total land area. Portugal claimed Brazil and parts of India. Japan held Korea and China, as well as the Philippines during the Second World War. The Dutch took charge of Indonesia and part of Taiwan. While these powerful nations shared certain methods and philosophies, it is important to note that colonizers differed in their use of force, treatment of native populations, and the degree to which they demanded assimilation to metropolitan standards and culture.

It is no coincidence that the heyday of European colonialism/imperialism coincided with a burgeoning capitalist economy, which required both raw materials and human labor to fuel production and consumption. Modern colonialism/imperialism didn't just conquer foreign lands, it created new economic systems in which human and material resources flowed between colony and metropolis. The economies of the colonies became inextricably linked to the economy of the colonizing nation.[4] Many of the earliest settlements centered around trading companies sponsored by colonizing nations, including the British East India Company, Hudson's

---

4. Loomba, *Colonialism/Postcolonialism*, 3.

Bay Company, the French East India company, and the Dutch East India Company.

Decolonization

The colonies that eventually became the United States gained independence from Britain in 1776 following the Revolutionary War. Canada's nationhood was established in 1867, although some provinces did not join the Dominion of Canada until the mid-twentieth century. By the beginning of the First World War, nine-tenths of the earth's surface was under imperial control and/or occupation, and one-quarter of the world population was under the influence of the British Empire. The era post-World War II witnessed colonized peoples reclaiming power and control in a relatively rapid process of decolonization, as many colonized peoples, including most of Africa, claimed independence from their former colonizers. There were a number of reasons for decolonization, including resistance from colonized peoples, supported by the USSR, China, and Cuba; the rising cost of maintaining colonies; and pressure from the United States, which viewed colonial trading policies as barriers to its own expansion of trade. This is evidence of the growing global influence of the United States post-WWII. Despite achieving independence, the power of former colonies was often nominal and could only be exercised within the context of Western capitalism. For example, Africa was rich in resources, but the markets and channels for distributing such resources were located elsewhere, and governments were forced to maintain the economic relationships of their former colonizers. Thus, some nations regained political power but not economic power.

Another consequence of decolonization has been the tendency of native leaders to mimic the former colonizers, so that newly independent states emerge "fully cloaked in the colonial garment and devoted to the structures and policies of their former colonizers."[5] For the United States and Canada, independence did not end the process of claiming land. As the nations expanded westward, there was a continued struggle against the aboriginal inhabitants for land occupancy and ownership. Ironically, both newly independent nations mimicked forceful colonizing practices by seizing land and attempting to "civilize" existing populations. National railway systems literally cut through lands that others claimed as home. As the historian Kariann Yakota argues, post-revolutionary Americans,

5. Dube, "Postcoloniality, Feminist Spaces and Religion," 101.

especially the elite, were anxious to maintain at least cultural ties with the British Empire: "the importation of material culture, ideas and experts from the mother country was an integral part of a provincial people's attempt to construct a 'civilized' nation on the periphery of the transatlantic world."[6] Thus, American nation-building was a complex mix of emulation and separation. The new country realized it still hovered on the margins of power and needed to cultivate a positive social and economic relationship with its former parent.

Civilizing Mission

Toward the end of the nineteenth century, social Darwinism and other theories provided theoretical justification for the domination of one race over another, thus constructing colonialism as a necessary and natural act resulting in the civilizing or betterment of the colonized peoples. This perceived responsibility is what Rudyard Kipling called the "White Man's burden." In 1909, Canadian professor George M. Wrong wrote: "Britain controls today the destinies of some 350,000,000 alien people, unable as yet to govern themselves, and easy victims to rapine and injustice, unless a strong arm guards them."[7] The unjust processes of colonialism were obfuscated behind "a liberal smokescreen of civilizing 'task' and paternalistic 'development' and 'aid.'"[8] Recently, such an attitude has been termed the White Saviour Industrial Complex, referring to a tendency for wealthy white individuals to put tremendous resources toward "making a difference" in the lives of the poor and disadvantaged, without adequate research or consultation with those experiencing need.[9]

The means and methods of colonial subjugation are both physical and psychological. By portraying others negatively, Western colonizers have continually underlined their own superiority. In 1978, Edward Said published *Orientalism*, which draws on Marxist theories of power to reflect on the way colonizers produce knowledge about colonies in a manner that justifies their subjugation. Western production of knowledge about the "Orient" (Said refers mainly to the Middle East and Egypt) has perpetuated stereotypical representations of the Eastern peoples, including the idea that

6. Yokota, *Unbecoming British*, 9.

7. Berger, *The Writing of Canadian History*, 11.

8. Ashcroft et al., *Post-Colonial Studies*, 57.

9. Cole, "The White Saviour Industrial Complex."

the Orient is "timeless," unchanging, fantastic, bizarre, and that its people are variously degenerate.[10] According to Said, Western representations are founded upon unequal binary divisions according to which the Orient is constructed as the opposite of the West. The "West occupies a superior rank while the Orient is its 'other,' in a subservient position."[11] In the decades of imperial expansion, the West "accumulated experiences, territories, peoples, histories; it studied them, classified them, verified them, and above all, it subordinated them to the culture and indeed the very idea of white Christian Europe."[12] The non-European world served conveniently as the constitutive "other" for Europe's dominant image of itself as rational and civilized. Increasingly, the colonized "other" existed to define the colonizer as culturally and morally superior. This tendency became more pronounced throughout the eighteenth century, as Germany, the Netherlands, Belgium, France, and England expanded their colonial domains, and as scientific and technological advances of the enlightenment placed the West in a position of significant advantage over the rest of the world.

Christianity and Civilizing Mission

The Christian church in the West advocated and participated in these projects of civilizing mission. According to Canadian theologian Marilyn Legge, "Christianity has been an essential part of global imperial social ordering, regularly and morally legitimating the mechanisms of controlling markets and raw materials to exploit the colonies and their populations."[13] European empires planted populations of white settlers in lands already occupied by indigenous populations, resulting in displacement as well as physical and cultural genocide. This systematic destruction was generally taken for granted by church hierarchies and missionary departments. At times, churches participated in destruction of other cultures by inserting Western Christian values into the lives of "savages" and insisting on the primacy of Western theological interpretations. The participation of the church in colonial projects, or its tolerance of them, was often justified by a type of conquest theology that is "a central aspect of a colonial and imperialistic mentality that continues to generate dualistic divisions between 'us'

10. Said, *Orientalism*, 96.
11. McLeod, *Beginning Postcolonialism*, 41.
12. Said, "Yeats and Decolonization," 72.
13. Legge, "Negotiating Mission," 122.

and 'them' while claiming that 'God is on our side' as a way to justify acts of aggression and power."[14] Matthew 28:19 and other biblical texts have been used as scriptural warrants for these conquests. It can be difficult to untangle the "Christianizing mission" of the church from the "civilizing mission" of Western colonizers. Both have ascribed superiority to Western cultural institutions, "portraying the West as the center of all cultural good, a center with a supposedly redemptive impulse, while it relegates all other cultures to the project of civilizing, Christianizing, assimilating, and developing."[15] Interpreted through Western imperial eyes, the Bible itself has been used as a potent weapon of colonial power, justifying the conquest of land and populations.

For North American Christians, a particularly poignant example of civilizing mission is the cooperation among certain churches and governments regarding aboriginal children. In order to instill European-Christian values in children, residential schools were operated by missionaries and governments. Children were separated from their families, culture, and language. While residential schools were seemingly similar to one another in their cultural imperialism, some were implicated in dramatic and horrific physical, sexual, and emotional abuse. For these children and their families, the action of the church in cooperation with the governments of Canada and the United States have resulted in a lifetime of pain and a sense of dislocation from their own native cultures.

Western mission projects have benefited from colonial/imperial infrastructures. It was easier for churches to gain access to mission fields in regions that were under the control of a Western nation. "The missionaries from Europe and North America came out of a context that assumed the supremacy of Western Culture and 'Western religion,' that is, Christianity, in a single breath."[16] Missionaries did not generally question this system. It is important to remember, however, that there were thousands of missionaries sent out from various nations to perform tasks including evangelism, but also as institution builders: nurses, doctors, engineers, and teachers. They were not simply agents of empire, but often devoted and faithful servants seeking to do the will of God as they understood it. Some were also victims of an imperial machine insofar as they had little choice but to work within the existing political framework. Similarly, the recipients of Western

14. Peters, "Decolonizing our Minds," 93–110.

15. Dube, "Postcoloniality," 104.

16. Bevans and Schroeder, *Constants in Context*, 230.

missionary endeavors variously welcomed, tolerated, or resisted the offerings of the missionaries. Those who arrived with the goal of missionizing and civilizing were not left unchanged by their travels. In many cases, both native and foreigner were changed by one another.

Despite the serious questions raised by the unquestioned intrusion into other lands and cultures, the missionary movement has borne fruit, resulting in improvements and benefits for colonized persons. For example, in India the Christian mission often targeted tribal populations that were severely oppressed by the existing caste systems. For these converts to Christianity their newly acquired faith gave them a sense of worth and an opportunity for medical care and education that were otherwise inaccessible. In some areas, the presence of female missionaries offered native women a glimpse of women's potential that exceeded their imagination. Yet in other areas, the patriarchal nature of Christianity undermined matrilineal systems and resulted in a diminution of power for some women, along with increased subordination.[17]

Contemporary Manifestations of Empire

Fernando Segovia identifies the widespread presence of colonialism as: "an omnipresent, inescapable and overwhelming reality in the world," ancient and modern.[18] Although the twentieth century was a period of colonial demise, anticolonial struggles continue in many parts of the world, including East Timor, Tibet, Palestine, and the West Bank. Robert Young identifies a surprising number of regions that are still subordinate to powerful nations, including "British Gibraltar, the Falklands/Malvinas, Danish Greenland; Dutch Antilles, French Guiana, Martinique, Reunion, St. Pierre and Miquelon, US Puerto Rico, Samoa, Virgin Islands; Spanish Ceuta, Melilla, and the Canary Islands."[19] While the implanting of settlements that characterized modern colonialism is diminished in practice, and the imperial holdings are much smaller, "imperialism continues apace as Western nations such as America [sic] are still engaged in imperial acts, securing wealth and power through the continuing economic exploitation of other nations."[20] Global

---

17. Walls, "Missionary Societies," 154.

18. Segovia, "Biblical Criticism and Postcolonial Studies," 56.

19. Young, *Postcolonialism*, 3.

20. McLeod, *Beginning Postcolonialism*, 8.

superpowers continue to operate imperialistically, yet the primary means of control have changed dramatically since the mid-twentieth century.

Colonialism as the implanting of settlements has been superseded by neocolonialism, a term that denotes "a continuing economic hegemony that means the postcolonial state remains in a situation of dependence on its former masters, and that former masters continue to act in a colonist manner toward formerly colonized states."[21] This dependence is not limited to economics but extends to military, psychological, and cultural arenas. One might point to global institutions such as the World Bank and International Monetary Fund as well as political initiatives such as the G8/G20 summits, which allow powerful nations to make decisions that affect the world at large. Industries such as mining frequently occupy the space of others in order to extract natural resources. These activities, even when well compensated, take a toll on the environment and the people of a given territory. In the United States, the economic disparity between black and white citizens can be at least partially attributed to the historical disparity between these groups. In Canada, there is similar disparity between aboriginal peoples and the population at large.

Globalization refers to the manner in which local communities and individuals are impacted by global economic and cultural forces. In the past century, the social relations of nations have been reorganized, reflecting the interdependency of economic markets and communication systems. Proponents of globalization perceive it as a positive phenomenon that increases local access to cultural and material global commodities, resulting in an improved standard of living for global communities. Opponents reject globalization "as a form of domination by 'First World' countries over 'Third World' ones, in which individual distinctions of culture and society become erased by an increasingly homogeneous global culture, and local economies are more firmly incorporated into a system of global capital."[22] This negative perception of globalization assumes that it is controlled by global power centers, and is another way in which the "center" regains power over "periphery."

While I perceive the term "globalization" to be somewhat neutral in itself, I acknowledge that in a postcolonial context globalization is not equally beneficial for all communities. From an ecclesiological perspective, while globalization can be associated with cultural imperialism and a

---

21. Young, *Postcolonialism*, 45.

22. Ashcroft et al., *Post-Colonial Studies*, 108.

tendency to homogenize ecclesial cultures, it also has the positive effect of increasing the potential for more intimate encounters with global others. The global media and increased mobility are examples of the manner in which globalization brings us closer to others literally and figuratively.[23]

Hallmarks of Colonizing Discourse

Colonialism/imperialism is at heart a relational system. It concerns the manner in which strong nations relate to weak nations, superior groups relate to inferior groups, how one group, nation, or class of people relates to another. Colonial discourse theory describes the complex web of verbal, written, and symbolic interactions among all those involved in colonial processes. This discourse is in no way one-sided. Colonized populations have responded to colonizers in a variety of ways in a variety of situations. Those who have been pushed to the margins find ways to talk back to the center. While I have briefly highlighted some of the past and present realities of empire, there are several characteristics that are highly instructive for understanding the complex relationships among center and periphery. Without losing track of the diversity of ways in which colonialism/imperialism has been practiced in different times and places, the following categories describe the manner in which empires, small and large, have sought to manage relationship and maintain power and control. The boundaries between categories are intended to be highly porous rather than restrictive, and one category frequently overflows into others.

Domination

Colonialism/imperialism has often taken the form of a violent dialogue among representatives of European states and the indigenous people of other continents. Despite a rhetoric of paternalistic benevolence, despite the imperial argument that colonial intrusion is for the good of the colonized population, colonizers have gone to great lengths to ensure their authority and control. Colonizers have unilaterally imposed culture and political rule without regard for the agency or autonomy of colonized peoples. Slavery and indentured labor movements, apartheid, military responses to colonial

23. For a Christian ethical analysis of globalization, see Peters, "The Future of Globalization," 105–33.

uprisings, sexual violence against indigenous women—all of these are examples of the violent tactics and consequences of colonialism/imperialism. The violence of slavery is a particularly poignant example of the manner in which human bodies were violated as a means of economic gain. By absolutely denying the autonomy, worth, even the humanity of enslaved persons, colonizers have sought to dominate and destroy souls and bodies.

In order to maintain power and control, colonizers have sometimes relied on visible military presence. The military may be a symbolic attempt to retain order and remind indigenous populations of their place in the hierarchy of the colony, or they may transcend the boundaries of ordinary policing, resulting in acts of unspeakable horror. An example is the Jallianwala Bagh massacre that took place in 1919 in Amritsar, India. In that instance, a British officer ordered fifty soldiers to fire on a crowd of approximately ten thousand Indians, resulting in the death of several hundred unarmed people. In a cycle of reciprocal violence, resistance to colonial force has frequently led to violent revolution—including the American Revolution. Often this takes the form of nationalist organizations that organize in order to regain independence, sometimes using violent means, sometimes seeking diplomatic solutions. In some situations, colonized peoples may begin to understand their own existence as a matter of violent confrontation with colonizing settlers.

Material consequences arising from the colonial oppression and exploitation of indigenous resources, such as poverty and food insecurity, are other forms of violence that threaten the physical well-being of colonized peoples. Domination, however, is not limited to the physical or material. Colonizers seek to dominate colonies in more symbolic ways. "It is not (just) the sword that establishes and maintains colonial authority but the culture of fear that violence produces and depends upon."[24]

Colonial/imperial powers also attempt to control the production of knowledge about colonized peoples. Representations, images, and ideas about colonized people and cultures are created and disseminated without their input or participation, often resulting in inaccurate and degenerate portraits of the colonized others.[25] Colonizers have relied on stereotypes to describe the identities of the colonized peoples: "laziness, aggression, violence, greed, sexual promiscuity, bestiality, primitivism, innocence and irrationality are attributed (often contradictorily and inconsistently) by

---

24. Jefferess, *Postcolonial Resistance*, 124.

25. McLeod, *Beginning Postcolonialism*, 22.

the English, French, Dutch, Spanish and Portuguese colonists to Turks, Africans, Native Americans, Jews, Indians, the Irish, and others."[26] A strategy of colonizing imagination has been employed by colonizers in order that colonized subjects might view themselves according to colonial representations. In this sense, colonizing discourse has interfered with the right of colonized peoples to narrate their own histories and identities. The narrative of colonial power has left little room for the oppressed to speak: "they exist only as they are constructed within the colonial imagination, a function of the empire's will to power."[27]

By insisting upon the intellectual, political, economic, technological, and spiritual superiority of the West, Western powers have constructed a world order that situates themselves at the center and pushes all others to the margins. Decisions regarding the lives and livelihoods of colonized peoples have been made by others who lived in distant lands, or who have resided, unwelcome, in the colonies. The lives, possessions, and land of colonized persons have been dominated, without their permission and against their will, by others who have perceived an inherent right to seize what does not in fact belong to them.

Separation

Colonizing discourse constructs oppositional relationships between colonized and colonizer. The power of one group over another forces the maintenance of social boundaries. Postcolonial theorists such as Homi Bhabha have posited that colonists separate "civilized" and "savage" in order to maintain cultural purity. However, Bhabha contests the very existence of cultural purity, contending that all cultures are mixtures, or hybrids. In order to uphold their own superiority and "right to rule," colonizers insist on the existence of cultural purity and avoid mixedness by maintaining social and physical boundaries between rulers and ruled. "Different colonial regimes tried (to varying extents) to maintain cultural and racial segregation precisely because, in practice, the interactions between colonizing and colonized peoples constantly challenged any neat division between races and cultures."[28] For example, servants of color worked within white households or natives were employed as civil servants to work under and among

26. Loomba, *Colonialism/Postcolonialism*, 107.

27. Jefferess, *Postcolonial Resistance*, 24.

28. Loomba, *Colonialism/Postcolonialism*, 69.

colonial agents. As different groups were brought into proximity, it called into question the identities and stereotypes manufactured and relied upon by colonizing power. Were colonized populations really as fundamentally different, inferior to their colonial masters?

In order to justify colonial/imperial projects, it has been important to emphasize differences among rulers and ruled. Thus, the practice of overemphasizing differences has been used as a weapon of oppression. Letty Russell has written, "essentializing declares that differences of race, sex, class, and sexual orientation are part of created nature and cannot be changed. When we essentialize, it is possible to justify oppression, poverty, exploitation, and imperialism by declaring that the dominating group has been created to 'rule the world.'"[29] As noted above, colonizers have sought to construct the identity of those whom they have oppressed, which has served to legitimate and rationalize European oppression, insofar as colonial subjects have been constructed as a threat to the security of the empire, or as needing external governance (i.e., they have been constructed as children in need of parenting, or uncivilized). For example, colonial leaders have monitored the sexual relationships of colonized peoples and expressed considerable anxiety around relationships among colonized and colonizers. This anxiety may have arisen from a fear that colonizers would "mix" with indigenous cultures, undermining claims to cultural superiority and "blurring the line" between ruler and ruled.[30] An example of the church aiding the preservation of an unjust status quo in order to protect the security of imperial interests arises from missionary hermeneutics. Sugirtharajah has argued that commentaries written during the colonial period for the Anglican Church in India "seek out and identify what they deem to be evils of Indian society: superstition, mendacity, laziness and bribery; all of these have to be resisted. In setting moral boundaries between Indian Christians and other Indians, the commentaries served to establish the case for British intervention. By prescribing Christian morality, these commentaries become the textual means for justifying the British occupation as the harbinger of civilization."[31] This kind of separation was not enforced by all colonizers. Some, including the Portuguese in India and the Spanish in

---

29. Russell, "Cultural Hermeneutics," 37.

30. Streets, "Gender and Empire."

31. Sugirtharajah, "Imperial Critical Commentaries," 87–88.

America, preferred to settle in the colony, intermarrying and adopting local language and customs, thus providing "a strong base for colonial rule."[32]

It has been in the best interest of colonizers to enforce "divide and rule" policies, which emphasize differences among subgroups within a particular colony. An extreme example of colonial separation is the apartheid policies of South Africa. Apartheid is a politic of separation that divided people according to race, and thus prevented contact and preempted the possibility of cultural understanding. Another example of separation that divides a native population stems from the tendency of colonizers to deploy natives as agents of colonial power. These natives acted as intermediaries to ensure that colonizers did not have to come face to face with oppressed populations. In other cases, indigenous landowners have cooperated with colonial leaders in order to protect their own interests, a practice that sometimes had negative consequences for those who tenanted the land.

Despite these attempts at separation, ironically the colonized and colonizers are inextricably linked with one another. Historically, colonizers have not been able to manage the land and exploit natural resources without the labor and knowledge of indigenous populations. At the same time, the colonized are forced to depend upon their colonial masters for employment and safety.

In the postcolonial era, there are still attempts to separate persons and groups from one another. The manner in which market forces extend and drive the gap between rich and poor is one example. In Canada, First Nations populations are still relegated to reserve lands. In the United States, segregation between white and black Americans continues unofficially, even in the absence of legislation requiring segregation.

Homogeneity

At the heart of empire is a contradiction. While colonialism/imperialism has sought to maintain boundaries between persons and groups, it has also aimed to erase otherness in a quest for unity and homogeneity. Murder, genocide, and ethnic cleansing are extreme manifestations of a drive to erase difference or otherness. By suppressing indigenous systems in favor of Western governance, values, and culture, Western colonialism/imperialism has attempted to eradicate other cultures. It has been marked by a tension that sought both to separate groups by emphasizing "racial hierarchies in

32. Loomba, *Colonialism/Postcolonialism*, 110.

27

order to maintain rule and continue material exploitation," and simultaneously enforce a homogenous worldview by uplifting "primitive" groups to European "civilization."[33] While colonizers essentialized differences between and among people, they simultaneously attempted to unify disparate groups under a common flag, religion, or economic system. Colonial attempts to bridge the gap between province and metropolis have been rooted in an assumption that the worldview of the dominant culture is universal and can be held true for all humanity. "In the practice of colonialism, the universal human was revealed to be the white man."[34]All other cultures have been expected to fall in line behind the flag, religion, and economic system of the white man. Thus, other cultures have been undervalued or despised, and perceived to be in need of betterment or advancement.

The role of the historical Christian mission has been to bring about both religious and cultural homogeneity. In many of its modern missionary endeavors, the Christian church has revealed an "allergy to difference," placing little or no value upon indigenous religions or cultural systems.[35] Missionaries, as agents of cultural imperialism, have taught Western values and lifestyles. New converts to Christianity have been expected to conform to Western standards of dress, hygiene, and manners.

A contemporary example of homogenization arises from the hegemony of neoliberal economic globalization. Global economic institutions, such as the World Bank and the International Monetary Fund, and transnational corporations can be interpreted as an attempt to unify all markets under one Western economic model. All nations and peoples are expected to submit to the logic and order of Western economics.

Fixedness

Colonial/imperial projects have relied on the presentation of a stable and unified worldview rooted in the colonizer's right to rule and control colonized peoples. This concept of fixedness is closely related to the suppression of difference, separation, and boundary maintenance described above. By fixing boundaries and social roles, colonizing discourse has kept groups separate from one another. Colonizers have worked to convince colonized

---

33. Silverstein and Barrows, "Colonialism."

34. Jefferess, *Postcolonial Resistance*, 34.

35. Keller et al., *Postcolonial Theologies*, 10.

peoples that the language of empire is normative—the true order of life.[36] "Under colonialism, a colonized people are made subservient to ways of regarding the world which reflect and support colonialist values. A particular value system is taught as the best, truest world-view."[37] Thus, colonizing discourse seeks to fix identities and social relationships into a hierarchy of categories such as ruler/ruled, colonizer/colonized, and civil/savage. Modern colonial/imperial processes have been fixed within a Western, Christian metanarrative, which assigned roles and established boundaries between and among peoples. Class systems are prime examples; classes assign individuals or groups a particular identity based on their position within a fixed hierarchy of categories. Movement between classes, or mixing of classes, is discouraged or forbidden.

Religious, social, and political systems claiming that language, knowledge, and boundaries are fixed may be aesthetically pleasing, and may offer a sense of security because they are without loose ends, troubling inconsistencies, or ambiguities. Such systems provide the framework for ideologies that claim to have no alternative.[38] There is thus room for only one story, one version of reality, one construction of social relationships. Everything has been decided, and thus there is little freedom of moment or room for change. Such logic locks colonized persons into a subservient position with no recourse. Some are created to rule, others are created to obey.

Conclusion

Our lives are played out on the stage of empire. While *colonizing discourse* may not be a familiar term for most, it is a familiar discourse. We are accustomed to a world in which some dominate, in which some people should be kept apart from others, in which homogeneity is valued over diversity, in which there is a preference for one, single worldview. At the same time, our lived reality challenges the precepts of colonizing discourse. An unintended yet infinitely valuable side effect of empire has been hybridity. In enforcing a single way of life, European colonialism/imperialism ultimately brought about a world characterized by the mixing of all peoples and nations. In North America, we are "in-between," a complex and layered culture that is neither East nor West, North nor South. It is no longer simple to define the

36. McLeod, *Beginning Postcolonialism*, 19.
37. Ibid.
38. World Alliance of Reformed Churches, "Accra Confession," para. 10.

demographic of our local communities nor the broader community within which we preach the word of God. Culture is blurry and messy. The neatly defined boundaries of colonizing discourse will not ultimately hold us. In the words of Trinh T. Minh-ha, "despite our desperate, eternal attempt to separate, contain, and mend, categories always leak."[39] Yet colonizing discourse continues to wreak havoc within our local and global relationships. In what ways is our pulpit discourse vulnerable to the insistent voice of colonialism/imperialism? In what specific ways does the world history of colonialism/imperialism that has been described in this chapter contribute to the complexity of the preaching arena? I now turn to the postcolonial context of today's pulpit.

39. Minh-ha, *Other*, 94.

2

The Challenge of Preaching in the Midst of Empire

Understanding the Context

NORTH AMERICA IS A postcolonial space. Nowhere is this more visible and tangible than in an international airport. After a long journey from Managua, Nicaragua, I returned home to Toronto. In the crowded customs and immigration hall, it seemed as though planes from every corner of the globe had landed simultaneously. Waiting in line to present my documents to a customs agent, I had plenty of time to consider the other new arrivals. Like me, they appeared travel-worn and ready to be finished with the official business of entering Canada. Some passengers chattered excitedly, while some murmured anxiously. A cacophony of languages blended into one another: I thought I could identify Spanish, French, Italian, Korean, and Hindi. In my jet-lagged state, I had a momentary sense of disorientation. Where was I? Which country? The boundaries of race, nationality, and ethnicity blurred in this multinational space. Languages, histories, and identities were unclear; familiar categories were not applicable. Such is the disorientation of living in a globalized, hybrid world. Although I have grown up in a multicultural country, I am still surprised at times by the challenge of adapting to diversity.

That day at the airport my sense of disorientation was accompanied by a sense of pride about the easy tolerance and multiculturalism of my home country. All of the people waiting in this multilingual, multiethnic line held Canadian passports. This line was for citizens, not international visitors. A little voice in my head proclaimed "We are the world" in giddy recognition of my good fortune in being born in a place that is so welcoming and generous. This self-satisfaction lasted only a moment. My postcolonial training kicked in, and I recognized an imperial voice that sought to generously welcome others to "my country." I clung to the unacknowledged assumption that Canada is a white, Anglo-Saxon country benevolently making room for others. Canadians are extremely proud of their tolerance for diversity. This tolerance of otherness, however, is revealed as myth when it is measured against the real lives of immigrants and non-dominant groups, both historically and in the present. While it is tempting to uncritically celebrate diversity, it has been achieved at a great cost. A darker reality is concealed behind the rhetoric of tolerance. For those who have the luxury of doing so, it is much more comfortable to ignore or deny the elements of colonialism/imperialism and racism that have defined the past and intrude on the present.

With the exception of the aboriginal inhabitants of North America, all residents are immigrants: all have come from elsewhere at some point in the last several centuries. The original settlers were citizens or chattel of other empires—British, French, and Spanish. These empires planted settlements with little regard for aboriginal populations, importing disease and effectively destroying existing patterns of livelihood. Beyond these early settlers, immigrants from every corner of the planet have chosen to share life on this continent, resulting in tremendous cultural and ethnic diversity. Of course, not all chose to be here, not all came willingly. Some arrived on slave ships, others as refugees or displaced persons desperately seeking shelter in whichever nation would grant them access. Regardless of how and why these groups have come to live here, the constitution of the population is largely a consequence of modern colonialism/imperialism, which paved the way for people and goods to transverse the globe with relative ease. The development of North America has to some extent come about by means of violence, rape, systematic oppression, and the forced movement of groups from one continent to another. The benefits of cultural diversity and globalization are tremendous, but the colonial/imperial legacy is complex and has significant consequences for those of us who preach within this context.

Recent homiletic scholarship has highlighted the importance of the context in which preaching occurs. Preachers have been encouraged to develop an in-depth understanding of their own local context as well as broader social contexts. The preaching arena is multilayered, consisting of overlapping contexts: individual, local, regional, national, and global. In order to develop sermons that are sensitive to the life experience and perceptive tendencies of listeners, preachers take into account variables that define the identity and experience of individual listeners such as age, ethnicity, socioeconomic status, and sexual orientation. Each listener comes with a particular and unique set of experiences and identities that have been shaped by multiple factors. Leonora Tubbs Tisdale argues that a key role for preachers is that of ethnographer. In order to produce sermons that are meaningful and relevant, preachers must pay attention not only to individual identities, but to communal identity.[1] By recognizing the local symbols and stories that undergird the worldview and theologies of a given congregation, preachers will be able to engage the hearts and imaginations of the local church.

Mapping an understanding of listener contexts is becoming increasingly complex.

Preaching addresses both the particularities of the local congregation and the more general condition of the culture at large. The wider context includes all the forces that characterize culture and is comprised of both historical and contemporary realities. For example, preaching today addresses a social context that is moving from a modern to postmodern perspective and is increasingly shaped by rapid technological advancement and globalization. Local churches will experience these shared social realities in different ways depending on factors such as geography and social location, yet all are deeply affected by them.

Postcoloniality is one layer of the contemporary shared context. *Postcolonial* does not suggest that empire and colonialism/imperialism are safely located in the past, but suggests we continue to be affected by them. We are increasingly aware of these processes as significant historical and contemporary forces, and critical of the underlying assumptions and outcomes of these processes. Today, congregations are located in a space that has been and continues to be affected by the concerns of empire. In the previous chapter, I traced some of the historical and contemporary events and practices that were brought about by European colonialism/imperialism. These events and practices constitute a broadly shared history. However, there is a great deal of difference within and across congregations regarding

1. Tisdale, *Preaching as Local Theology*, 94.

experience of and participation in colonial/imperial projects. Depending on one's birthplace, family history, and life experiences one may identify with historically colonized and marginalized groups or with powerful, colonizing nations, or both. All are caught in a web of empire and, at least on the global stage, simultaneously play the roles of perpetrator and victim. As citizens of a nation with relative wealth and power, we unwittingly contribute to the oppression of others around the world. Some of us participate in the marginalization of certain groups within our own culture. Some are doubly or triply oppressed by virtue of race, gender, religion, or socioeconomic status. Even those occupying positions of tremendous privilege find it impossible to disentangle from the omnipresent web of empire that demands and requires participation.

This is an age of globalization, an age in which global cultures and markets are interconnected. A visit to the local shopping mall confirms this reality. Many of the goods available for purchase have been created and sourced on the other side of the world. Food courts display the culinary offerings of multiple cultures. North American financial markets are highly integrated with global markets. If there is a problem with the yen or the euro, it will affect the way that Americans do business. The morning after the 2012 presidential election, news sources worldwide expressed strong opinions on the reelection of President Barack Obama. In a globalized world, internal political decisions have far-reaching global consequences. This interconnectedness means that what happens here matters elsewhere, and vice versa.

The United States holds a great deal of influence on the global stage because of its economic, military, and cultural resources. As citizens of a powerful nation, American Christians find themselves in a position of power in relation to the rest of the world. Frequently, the government of the United States intervenes in the internal affairs of others as a means to protect its own interests and to monitor global security. Within its own borders, however, the United States is defined by deep and longstanding divisions of power. Some groups occupy the center, others are marginalized. The United States has both a history and an ongoing engagement with colonialism/imperialism. These factors create a cultural fabric shared by those who were born on American soil, and those who have chosen it as their home.

Christians in the West are adherents of denominations with particular histories and philosophies of mission and power. Western Christians, especially in partnership with various empires and cushioned by Christendom, have been on the leading edge of global religious power. Today, some churches and Christian organizations continue to hold a degree of social power. Many churches, however, find themselves unsure of their place in the social hierarchy. Where Christianity once occupied a central position of authority, this primacy is being called into question. Mainline churches are reporting declines in membership. This decline is especially noticeable in several denominations that have historically held a great deal of authority, including the Presbyterian Church (USA), American Baptist Church, and the Evangelical Lutheran Church in America.[2] As fewer Americans associate with mainline denominations, the remaining members may experience a sense of dislocation or homelessness. Biblical scholar and theologian Walter Brueggemann has employed the metaphor of "exile" to describe the contemporary situation of the Christian church. As the role of the church in public discourse is radically altered, the church finds itself exiled to a new and unknown territory. In short, Christianity is no longer the imperial religion, no longer occupying the center of power, no longer aligned with empire.[3] An increasingly marginalized church will require an alternative imagination if it is to thrive in this new context, lacking the protection and affirmation of the empire. There is a danger, however, that marginalization and a sense of homelessness may rapidly translate into insecurity. Theologian Charles Fensham warns that churches sensing a loss of power may be tempted to preserve their existing power at all costs, by hiding or ignoring power inequalities, suppressing difference, or cementing hierarchies.[4] This shifting landscape of ecclesial power is part and parcel of the postcolonial context.

A legacy of missionary activity and immigration is the increasing diversity of churches in the West. While individual congregations are frequently monocultural, national churches often attract adherents of varying race, ethnicity, and language. Some churches have no racial diversity, but some variety of ethnicity and national origin. These differences are accompanied by a diversity of theologies and attitudes about public issues. These and many other factors are examples of the shared context of preaching.

There are also aspects of lived reality that are shared by only some listeners or are uniquely experienced by individuals. These include skin

2. Lindner, *Yearbook of American and Canadian Churches*.

3. Brueggemann, *Hopeful Imagination*, 99.

4. Fensham, "The Glory of God Gives Life," 59.

color, primary language, and the number of generations that one's family has been at home in America. Cultural assumptions will vary among individuals depending on their unique history and the manner in which they have blended American cultural assumptions with the assumptions of their family or country of origin. Individuals retain pride in their ethnic and national heritage, sometimes resulting in a sense of cultural superiority or inferiority. Individuals will judge local and national governments based on their own priorities, politics, and background.

A postcolonial perspective on the context of preaching will acknowledge the variance of colonial/imperial experience and memory among worshippers. Some listeners belong to historically dominant cultures and have grown up without questioning the right of one group to dominate another. They may be immune to power dynamics or quite content to hierarchically view the world. Others have experienced firsthand what it is to be oppressed by a colonizer or have witnessed with their own eyes systems, such as apartheid, that are recent and horrifically visible symbols of separation politics. Many will wonder what a conversation about empire and colonialism has to do with them. Isn't it a thing of the past? Why should we bear responsibility for the actions of nations so long ago? Others will hunger for justice, for reparations, for apology, for forgiveness. Some cannot avoid the implications of power politics and marginalization related to the imperial complex because they are victims of ongoing injustice on a daily basis.

The space of worship is the space of the gathered community. It is also a space in which a variety of identities collide. Worshippers and worship leaders arrive with their individual, familial, and cultural identities intact. Those who gather share some aspects of identity related to their Christian and cultural identity, yet differ in significant ways. Imagine an urban, mainline protestant congregation: Trinity Presbyterian. In recent years, this congregation has experienced a membership decline, mostly due to the death of several elderly members and increasing professional mobility. The older members wistfully remember a time when the minister of the church held a prominent role in the community, but that no longer seems to be the case. As the neighborhood becomes more diverse, some members of this congregation are beginning to feel pushed to the margins. Some feel as though they are outnumbered by adherents of other religious groups in the community and wonder what happened to the time when their denomination held a great deal of influence and authority in politics.

Many kinds of families attend this church. There are single adults, families with young children, middle-aged parents whose children have left home, and several students from the nearby university. There is some ethnic and racial diversity among those in the pews. With the exception of two African American men, however, the leadership of this church is entirely white and of European origin. There is thus little diversity among decision makers. Among the worshippers, there is more diversity. Vashtee and Priya emigrated from Guyana nearly thirty years ago, and many of their extended family live near. They were both raised in a mission church back in Guyana. Maeve is a widow formerly from Belfast, Northern Ireland. Sitting in front of her is the Mehta family. Chitra's parents were born in India early in the twentieth century. Across the aisle is the Khan family from Pakistan with their daughter and two sons. They immigrated only two years ago. They have struggled this week because their daughter has been bullied at school, told to go "back to where she came from." An African American widower named James has chosen a pew near Janet, a white South African widow. At home, some of these families turn to CNN for updates on world events, some Fox, some ABC news. The preacher is an older woman, born in the Midwest, whose maternal grandparents were from England.

Consider the spaces among and between all these worshippers. Think about the colonial/imperial history and memory that binds them and separates them. What are the various positions of power held by individuals within the church and in their daily lives in relation to ethnicity, gender, race, language, or immigration status? Generally, power differentials and cultural difference are unspoken and unrealized. Consider the ways that these differences might affect how listeners will hear and participate in the sermon, or judge the authority of the preacher, or enter into relationship with the person seated next to them on a Sunday morning. While Trinity Church is a stylized example, it is suggestive of the potential diversity of congregations.

The aspects of lived experience I have just described are evidence of postcolonial situation. Worship spaces are inhabited by both (formerly) colonizing and (formerly) colonized peoples as well as observers, all of whom live in a nation that continues to be affected by imperial forces and participates in colonial discourses. To draw an example from church life in Canada, worshippers in established, mainline churches are often confronted with a collection of flags at the front of the worship space, including the Union Jack. When worshippers gather for coffee in the church hall after the service, a portrait of Queen Elizabeth II is a vivid reminder not only of Canada's membership in the British Commonwealth but also of Canada's colonial/imperial history. American churches often display American flags, not only symbols of national citizenship but also reminders of imperial power.

Sermons are preached and heard by persons living in the midst of empire, some of whom bear on their bodies and souls very real scars of colonial/imperial oppression, some of whom belong to groups that bear historic responsibility for such scars. All of them live in a nation that wields considerable economic, political, military, and cultural power in relation to the rest of the world. These people live in communities that are increasingly diverse ethnically and religiously. In the space between these persons, in the space between pulpit and pew, in the space between church and world beyond, there lies the possibility of trouble. As described in the previous chapter, colonialism/imperialism foster colonizing discourse. In the ecclesial space, colonizing discourse disrupts community and threatens the bond of Christian love. Beyond the ecclesial space, colonizing discourse disrupts the mission of God's church to reach out to both neighbor and stranger. What is the role of the pulpit in disrupting this discourse and participating in the decolonization of church and society?

The Postcolonial Pulpit

We preach in the interstices of empire. In a postcolonial society, empire is an ever-present reality, and creates a significant challenge for preachers. In this day and age, postcoloniality is an aspect of the broad context of listeners whether or not it is recognized and acknowledged by preachers. Acknowledgment is only the beginning of postcolonial engagement. There are significant benefits to incorporating postcolonial perspectives into homiletic practice. Preaching is a constructive and formative act. Over time, sermons contribute to the congregation's collective worldview, ethics, and identity. In attending to postcolonial reality, preachers open themselves to new possibilities for speaking a word of God that is relevant and appropriate to the lived reality of listeners. A carefully considered approach to the postcolonial situation can sharpen the transformative effects of sermons. One of the goals of this approach is to aid listeners in constructing a worldview attentive to the effects of empire, a profound and loving ethical engagement with a multiplicity of others, and an identity not limited to what the empire seeks to construct and endorse.

Worldview

The manner in which preachers approach the postcolonial situation has implications for the quality and truthfulness of preaching. While the purposes and expected outcomes of sermons will vary widely from preacher to preacher, most share a hope that the words of the sermon will be heard and resonate in some way with the lived experience of listeners. Preachers long for the word of God to inhabit the sermon so as to educate, illuminate, cause change, influence behavior, or comfort those who hear. The Holy Spirit, of course, takes the spoken words and uses them in ways the speaker might not expect or intend, and in doing so God participates fully in faith formation. Yet human words are fallible: they can fall flat, be open to misinterpretation, or, indeed, miss their intended target entirely. An awareness of empire, of colonial/imperial memory, of the omnipresence of empire in both biblical texts themselves and our interpretations of texts will aid preachers to address the world as it is while simultaneously imagining an alternative world. Scriptural interpretations will be more faithful, the grasp of our own contexts and the contexts of listeners will be more careful, and preachers will be able to speak a fuller truth. This is also true of the way preachers interpret the world in all its complexity. Postcolonial perspectives deepen insight into current events and enable a more vivid and multifaceted interpretation of history.

Ethics

The ethical implications of incorporating postcolonial perspectives into the practice of preaching are numerous. One task of preaching is to foster community and provide guidance for relationships among Christians and with others beyond the Christian community. The sermon participates in the shaping of the gathered people as an ethical community, lifting up biblical and theological models for human relationship and ethics. The manner in which preachers interpret Scripture, represent others, and respond to the claims of empire can affect the way listeners perceive and respond to others. Ronald Allen reminds us that "the preacher is called to help the congregation name how it responds to particular encounters with Others and to reflect on points at which the congregation's response is consistent with faithful theological convictions and points at which the congregation needs to reconsider its response to Others."[5]

Preaching fosters ethical engagement at a number of levels. As I have emphasized above, preaching may influence the formation of relationships within the worship space itself, among those gathered for worship. Where colonizing discourse arises among listeners or between listener and preacher, the sermon itself can contribute to decolonization and repair of broken relationships. Within the ubiquitous label *Western Christian*, there are groups that possess more or less symbolic power. Aboriginal Christians have been on the receiving end of colonial/imperial civilizing mission. Church members may be immigrants raised in missionary churches that were planted by Western missionaries, and have been taught to respect the primacy of the mother church. For example, mission work in nineteenth- and twentieth-century Korea has led to a large and thriving population of Korean Presbyterians in Canada and the United States. These churches, rooted in a language other than English and in an Asian culture, may experience a sense of inequality when compared with non-immigrant, English-speaking churches within the same denomination. This inequality, or marginalization, has serious implications for situations in which churches and church leaders must work together.

Each particular local Christian church relates to all other Christian churches. We are the body of Christ in the world, connected through word and sacrament across time and space. The biblical witness points to the normative values of equality and mutuality around Christ's table. Despite this egalitarian vision, the global church is fractured and prone to power dynamics. Christians live and work in highly diverse settings and possess variant degrees of power in relation to one another. This divide of power and influence is often geographical: western/eastern, northern/southern. At least some of this power difference can be attributed to the manner in which global mission has unfolded in previous centuries. Sending missionaries, often in full cooperation with empires, has resulted in church planting across the globe. Western churches today maintain relationships with these other churches, but the space between these younger and older churches is fertile ground for colonizing discourse. This is partly because of existing power inequalities and cultural assumptions, including cultural superiority, but especially because the establishment of these churches coincided with the era of westernizing civilizing mission. Beyond these international

5. Allen, *Preaching and the Other*, 34.

ecclesial bonds, North American churches are frequently engaged in aid, relief, and development work. This work may be represented or discussed in sermons in order to raise awareness of denominational partnerships and projects. Any time western preachers address issues around global mission, development, or poverty, there arises the potential for misrepresentation, paternalistic benevolence, and attitudes of cultural superiority.

As the population continues to diversify, the percentage of the population belonging to major world religions other than Christianity also increases. Here again arises the challenging issue of Christianity's shifting influence. Diana Eck perceives that increasing religious diversity has resulted in a "New Religious America." She notes that there are more Muslim Americans than Episcopalians or Presbyterians.[6] Post 9/11, colonizing discourse has emerged in the public rhetoric surrounding Muslim groups. Postcolonial perspectives may be helpful as Christians respond to the proximity of other religious groups, learning to coexist and even venturing into relationships of dialogue and mutual understanding.

More broadly, ethnic diversity has implications for community relationships. Preaching plays a potentially urgent role in fostering relationships among Christians and their immediate neighbors: on the soccer field, on the school playground, in the grocery store, and in the office. For example, the fastest growing population in the United States is Latino. But as Howard Recinos notes, "Latinos are viewed by too many of their neighbors as the disruptive outsiders who take jobs away from Americans, bringers of Latin America's social problems to U.S. soil, or simply strangers unwilling to adapt to U.S. society."[7] Preaching that highlights postcolonial themes and fosters a new perspective among listeners also influences the quality of relationships that listeners seek to form with those they live and work among. Postcolonial preaching enables listeners to consider this question: who is my neighbor? For example, how do disciples of Jesus Christ relate to First Nations peoples who continue to experience a sense of alienation and marginalization? What attitude is appropriate toward non-dominant groups? These are significant and difficult questions, especially for white Christians who are in the midst of experiencing a demographic shift and a resulting shift of culture and power.

Specifically in terms of church membership and the relationship among Christians within a single nation, we might wonder why the

---

6. Eck, *A New Religious America*.

7. Recinos, *Good News from the Barrio*, 5.

majority of churches are not reflective of the diversity of the country as a whole. Sunday morning remains the most segregated hour of the week. This monocultural tendency within some churches is a postcolonial issue insofar as it is deeply rooted in history, specifically in the history of modern colonialism/imperialism. Mutual mistrust has arisen in light of this history. The segregation of worship spaces involves the maintenance of boundaries and can be fueled by a desire to sustain cultural purity and avoid hybridity. The words of Harold Recinos apply just as well to the church as to American society at large: "society needs desperately to come to terms with its plural self, especially given that by the year 2050 white Americans will be a minority and people of colors will be in the majority."[8] What will this mean for the future church, and what is the role of the sermon in preparing for this emergent reality?

Identity: Individuals and Congregations

The preached word of God enables Christians to develop an understanding of who they are and the One to whom they belong. Both individual and collective identities are challenged, formed, and reformed through preaching. Listeners come to understand themselves as creatures in relationship to a loving God who sent Jesus Christ into the world to die and to rise again, as a people sustained and enabled by the Holy Spirit.

In a postcolonial era, the question of identity is key. Postcolonial literature and named experience highlight again and again themes of exile, belonging, and home. These themes are especially relevant for immigrants. As part of the diaspora, the great movement of persons across globe, home is increasingly difficult to define. There is fear that culture and language will be lost in a new land. There is loneliness and a sense of not quite belonging in the new location or the old. Of course, exile, belonging, and home are also highly relevant themes for those whose families have long and deep roots in America. Those whose families settled generations ago may experience a sense of disorientation similar to that which I identified in the opening anecdote about my experience at the airport. Boundaries are changing, perhaps becoming more permeable, which in turn creates a sense of disorientation. *Home* is evolving into something unfamiliar, no longer recognizable. For many, what has been perceived to be essential to American culture is being altered, resulting in calling into question long-established

8. Ibid.

social norms and values. Preaching assists Christians as they navigate this changing landscape, reminding listeners that Christian identity is rooted in the kingdom of God rather than the empires of this world. It raises the possibility that the margins, the in-between spaces in which nothing seems familiar, may be productive spaces where life can flourish. More specifically, postcolonial preaching leads listeners to reimagine home in a new way that is dependent not on the maintenance of boundaries or the securing of power but on self-giving love and openness to an unknown future.

The Pulpit and Colonizing Discourse

The practice of preaching is vitally important to the identity and ethics of the Christian church, yet, as with all institutions and practices in a postcolonial world, it is vulnerable to colonizing discourse. This discourse wheedles its way into sermons, unbidden and unwanted, dangerously unrecognized. Personal experience has alerted me to the need for postcolonial reflection on homiletic practice. As a white, privileged woman living in Canada, I have paid little attention to the impact of colonialism/imperialism in my life and in the lives of others. I have disregarded the implicit and explicit participation of the Christian church in colonial/imperial projects. Most disturbing are the moments when I am surprised to hear within my own voice a hint of colonizing discourse. Such discourse has emerged in the way I have represented others in my sermons, interpreted Scripture without paying adequate attention to the colonial/imperial background of the biblical text, or ignored the historical complicity of the Christian church with colonialism/imperialism, just to give a few examples.

In 2008, I traveled to a region of central India to which Canadian Presbyterians have sent missionaries for over one hundred years. This was my first experience of travel outside the West. I was fascinated and excited. I saw poverty that surpassed anything I had previously witnessed or imagined, and I jumped to all kinds of conclusions about what it means to "live well." I was disturbed because those "poor Indians" didn't live in the comfort I believed was essential for well-being. Eager to share my discoveries from the pulpit when I returned home, I was quick to plead for aid for that Indian community, citing a lack of hygiene, equipment, and expertise in the local hospital; a lack of desks and books in the school. All based on my assumption that we (the rich, Canadian church) needed to help, not only sharing material and financial resources, but also by sharing our superior expertise

43

and knowledge. My arrogant stance and cultural assumptions clearly reso-
nated with my listeners. After one sermon that referred to the hardships of
tribal Christians in India, a listener suggested that "we need to teach them
to be self-reliant." My listeners and I undervalued and mocked the agency,
autonomy, and abilities of our Indian friends. In complete ignorance of our
Western gaze, we sought to reshape them in our own image. And of course,
the assumption was that our financial gifts would be dependent on their
willingness to be shaped by our vision of who they ought to be.

After several visits to India and a foray into postcolonial literature,
I began to experience a new emotion: deep shame. Shame about some of
the attitudes toward others that I had exhibited. Shame for the uncritical
participation of my own denomination in mission projects that sometimes
demeaned the existing culture and identity of recipients. Shame for failing
to honor the value of other human beings, for overemphasizing my own
knowledge, for being a willing and uncritical agent of empire.

My preaching is not unique when it comes to mistakes and misrepresentations. Other preachers are similarly prone to colonizing discourse
in the preparation and delivery of sermons. This discourse might creep in
as we talk about foreign cultures or mission partners. It might creep in as
we reflect on the constitution of our neighborhoods or the actions of our
government. It enters sermons through our theologies, our biblical interpretations, and our cultural interpretations. In what ways might preaching
need to be decolonized? What follows is a discussion of just some of the
ways that the task of preaching is vulnerable to colonizing discourse.

Theology

Sermons communicate particular theological assumptions. The majority of
the theologies that underlie preaching in the Protestant mainstream have
been developed in the modern era. These theologies have grown, influenced, and been influenced by colonial/imperialist attitudes. While I share
Brian McLaren's reluctance to label the normative, standard theology of the
church as colonial, I am intrigued by his musing:

> What if we started calling standard, unmodified theology chau-
> vinist theology, or white theology, or consumerist, or colonial,
> or Greco-Roman theology? The covert assumption behind the
> modifier post-colonial thus becomes overt. . . . Standard, norma-
> tive, historic, so-called orthodox Christian theology has been

a theology of empire, a theology of colonialism, a theology that powerful people used as a tool to achieve and defend land theft, exploitation, domination, superiority and privilege.[9]

Postcolonial theologians wonder about the colonial/imperial roots and usages of modern theologies. While contemporary preachers have been influenced by postmodern theologies, many continue to operate using theological models that have not been examined for inherent assumptions about the nature of power, politics, or Western bias. Insofar as preachers have internalized these theologies, they will be reflected in sermons. I am not suggesting a rejection of standard or historic theologies but rather careful reflection about the inherent biases and assumptions of these theologies. Theologian Douglas John Hall reflects on the tendency of Christians in the West to inherently perceive their particular formulations of the Christian faith to be superior to all others.[10] Such an attitude is linked to the confidence of imperialistic Christendom, a world order that has placed Christianity at the top of an imagined religious and cultural hierarchy. A Christian faith in pursuit of power and glory must be called into question by those who recognize that such power and glory has come at great cost to many non-dominant and subaltern populations.

Cultural Assumptions

Preachers commonly draw examples and illustrations from personal and familiar sources. There lies the possibility that sermons reflect only one cultural perspective: that of the preacher. While preachers must take ownership of their own words and seek to be authentic, sermons are limited by a lack of conversation with others. When representing others in the preaching process, preachers and listeners may rely on assumptions and stereotypes about different groups and cultures. This may include overestimating knowledge about others and underestimating the agency and intelligence of others. If the world of the preacher is the only point of reference for the sermon, the preacher may unwittingly communicate that his or her own perspective is the only one that matters. A related assumption is that all people, everywhere, share the same perspective. The idea of a common, universal experience is a basic assumption of modernity. However,

9. McLaren, "Post-Colonial Theology."
10. Hall, *The Cross in Our Context*, 5–6.

the perspectives and experiences of different people, locally or globally, are characterized by tremendous diversity.

Preachers and listeners tend to underestimate the pervasiveness of empire in the world today and to assume that colonialism is a past and distant reality that has no effect in the present. Those from marginalized ethnic or cultural communities may be better able to articulate the manner in which colonialism/imperialism affect their own social location than those of European descent. The privileged social position of this latter group may mute their ability to critically reflect on issues such as neocolonialism, globalization, and the complicity of Western Christians in contemporary imperial projects. If preachers underestimate the pervasiveness of colonizing discourse or fail to recognize it altogether, they will be unable to speak out against it or to speak in favor of social and political systems that foster justice and equity. What is at stake is much more than mere intellectual resistance or assent to colonizing discourse. The emotional and material well-being of a multitude of others is affected by ongoing imperial reality and the destructiveness of colonizing discourse. Ignoring the effects of empire will also heighten the risk that the suffering of listeners and others beyond the church will also be ignored. Employing colonizing discourse in sermons unintentionally privileges some listeners and some segments of society over others.

Preachers and listeners, when confronted with the needs or limitations of others, especially those living in the Tricontinent,[11] are vulnerable to an attitude of paternalistic benevolence. Colonial/imperial powers have justified the subjugation of other peoples by claiming that external rule is necessary for the improvement, uplift, salvation, or civilization of colonized peoples. Such an attitude is motivated by a desire to help others and also a sense of cultural superiority: a belief that Western cultures, values, and infrastructures are superior, universally valid, and beneficial. When it comes to global ecclesial partnerships, or Western aid funding directed at the Tricontinent, preachers and listeners sometimes perceive a one-way relationship instead of a partnership of equals, as though these relationships consist only of knowledge and aid flowing from the West to the Tricontinent. Following one sermon in which I highlighted some of the positive and life-giving contributions of Canadian Presbyterians in India,

---

11. The Tricontinent refers to Latin America, Africa, and Asia. It was originally proposed during the meeting of the Organization of Solidarity of the Peoples of Africa, Asia and Latin America in Havana, 1966. Robert Young comments that "Tricontinental" avoids some of the pitfalls of the terms "Third World," the "South," and the "non-west."

one member of the congregation said "thank goodness for the British Empire, or those Indians would not have hospitals at all." This attitude reflects a belief that other cultures can only flourish with the intervention of Western nations. Western colonialism/imperialism has indeed had positive global effects, including advances in health care resulting in lower maternal and infant mortality, greater access to education, and participation in global trade. The Christian church today is truly global at least in part because of the doors opened by colonial/imperial systems. The wealth and knowledge of the West, however, does not supersede or invalidate the value of other cultures and communities. If sermons are to honor and fairly represent the lives of others, especially those living in poverty, then preachers will need to monitor their words for paternalistic and superior attitudes.

Preaching is vulnerable to colonizing discourse when it comes to biblical interpretation. The Bible contains the stories and experiences of colonized persons, yet the bulk of biblical translation and interpretation has been published by those associated with Western, colonizing nations. Biblical texts have been co-opted as partners in colonial/imperial projects and can potentially serve to justify imperial projects or even colonizing discourse. In addition, preachers today interpret biblical texts as postcolonial subjects with varying degrees of understanding or awareness of the past and continuing effects of colonial/imperial reality.

Colonizing discourse is chameleon-like. For many of us, it has become an integral part of our daily discourse, and we may not be able to easily recognize it in our own speech or that of others. Simply increasing awareness of the existence and pervasiveness of colonizing discourse will enable preachers to better respond whenever it arises in pastoral ministry. Beyond awareness, there are specific tasks to be undertaken by preachers wishing to banish colonizing discourse from their sermons.

Tasks of Decolonizing Preaching

Insofar as preachers and sermons are products of their cultural context, they are vulnerable to the lure of empire. Alternatively, preaching can participate in the process of "decolonizing the mind" by asking "how has the heritage of exploitation, privilege and prosperity shaped our identity as a people of faith?"[12] and by proclaiming a gospel that transcends and transforms discourses of power. Alerted to the presence of colonizing discourses

12. Peters, *Decolonizing our Minds*, 96.

in the ecclesial space and beyond, preachers can choose to speak against colonizing discourse and in favor of an ecclesial identity and ethical vocation more consistent with a community of faith that is created in the image of God.

What are the tasks associated with decolonizing preaching? These include recognizing difference and diversity within the listening community and beyond, naming colonialism/imperialism as a past and present reality, speaking against the damaging and destructive patterns and discourses that have emerged within colonial/imperial projects, and coming to terms with the relationship between church and empire. In order to combat the clear and present danger of misunderstanding among those with different backgrounds and colonial/imperial memory, preaching has the opportunity to construct a space in which understanding might flourish. Sermons themselves can play a role in bringing about reconciliation among parties that have been torn asunder by colonial/imperial violence. By adopting a form of biblical exegesis that attends to the colonial/imperial themes in the text and in the life of the interpreter, preachers retrain listeners to hear Scripture more accurately within its original context and locate resources for responding to empire today. Perhaps most importantly, preaching proclaims a new reality based in God's own nature and God's intention for human life and community. The future is not simply an outgrowth of the past. A postcolonial imagination enables both preachers and listeners to envision a world free from colonizing discourse. These tasks will be explained and explored throughout the remaining chapters.

None of these tasks will be easily accomplished. Decolonizing preaching requires a certain degree of comfort with ambiguity, as postcolonial problems are rarely clear cut and postcolonial responses resist simple categorization. Mark Lewis Taylor wonders where postcolonial theologies will possibly gain a foothold in American Christianity, when Christian groups appear "toothless and compliant" in the face of their nations aggressive imperialism.[13] Even as preachers attempt to utter a "no" to colonizing discourse, they continue to inhabit colonizing structures. Gayatri Spivak, a leading postcolonial scholar, terms this "neocolonial anticolonialism."[14] All of these challenges require preachers to practice a high degree of self-critique, as well as engage in a critique of the ecclesial and theological structures that are so familiar and well loved.

13. Taylor, "Spirit and Liberation," 163.
14. Spivak, *A Critique of Postcolonial Reason*, 191.

Conclusion

So far, I have explored some aspects of the context for North American preaching and considered how preaching is shaped by, and responds to, its postcolonial situation. Postcolonial reality constitutes a considerable challenge and opportunity for contemporary preaching. In order to develop a response to this challenge, preachers will benefit from both theological and philosophical resources. The field of postcolonial studies has produced a sustained and varied critique of colonialism/imperialism. Preaching, however, is primarily concerned with the word of God and proclaiming God's action in the world. Postcolonial theory is able to inform the practice of preaching, yet it does not offer a theological foundation for Christian identity and ethics. Formulations of the Social Trinity, however, reveal that God's life in Trinity has implications for both human social and political realities. A basic understanding of both postcolonial theories and Trinitarian theologies will equip preachers with a deeply reflective and constructive basis for decolonizing preaching.

PART II

Developing an
Alternative Discourse

3

A Theological Response to Empire

THE ETHOS OF EMPIRE is so deeply ingrained in modern consciousness there is barely room to consider alternative systems. Various
constructions and conceptions of the divine have contributed to,
and been shaped by, imperial worldviews. Christian theology has often
been limited to the insight of Western theologians and reflective of Western theological interpretation and practices. In this context of Western
theological imperialism, global voices are frequently marginalized and
struggle to be heard amid the historical din of academic theology in Europe
and North America. In that sense, the practice of theology itself has been
colonized, claimed, and exploited by dominant cultures. At the same time,
fruitful modes of theological inquiry have arisen all over the world, and
despite the dominance of Western theology, it is by no means the only, nor
most lively, location for the production of theological insight. At the very
least, European and North American theologies (indeed all theologies)
should be approached with a hermeneutic of suspicion, while leaving room
for the voices situated in colonized, or formerly colonized, locales. These
voices frequently contain an overt or subtle critique, even condemnation,
of colonialism/imperialism. Western theological methods will need to accept chastisement as a means to further faithful inquiry.

If we are to begin to imagine an alternative discourse, an alternative
system that has the potential to decolonize the earth, theology is an essential conversation partner. This is especially true when it comes to the
task of decolonizing preaching, which calls for a theo-ethical approach. The
practice of preaching is a deeply theological endeavor. It is a public naming
of God's nature, an ongoing public reflection on the relationship among

theology and anthropology. Preaching names who we are as a community, as well as what we might become in light of God's will and desire for the created order.

Colonialism/imperialism are sociopolitical realities that affect Christian identity and negatively impact local and global relationships within the church and beyond. The practices of colonialism and the ideology of imperialism problematize the participation of humanity in the fellowship of God as Creator, Son, and Holy Spirit, as well as distorting human relationships by discouraging or attempting to forbid discourses of love and friendship. The life of God-in-Trinity provides a theological foundation both for a constructive reimagining of human relationships damaged by colonizing discourse and for the deconstruction of colonizing discourse. Beyond merely interrupting or resisting colonial/imperial power, postcolonial preaching that is committed to a Trinitarian vision of God can proclaim the possibility of transformation through divine intervention.

Throughout the centuries, theologians have put forward different formulations of what it means for the One, Holy God to exist as three persons in community. Interpreted from a Trinitarian perspective, Scripture presents perspectives on God's action in the world that can be characterized according to the work of three divine persons. Creator, Son, and Spirit act in synchronicity, yet occupy different roles and purposes in salvation history. The Trinity has been and continues to be a central doctrine of the Christian church, yet it is a challenging concept to define and comprehend. In essence, the doctrine of the Trinity is an attempt to imagine God's nature, particularly as God is in relationship with the created order. There is a profound connection between our imagining of God's nature and our vision for human community. The manner in which human beings understand God's inner being and nature has significant consequences for how we imagine our own being and nature. Jürgen Moltmann, for example, claims that the manner in which human beings understand, image, and relate to God will impact their construction of human identities and ethics. In other words, how we perceive God influences who we are (identity) and how we behave toward others (our ethics). A community of faith will, to a certain extent, pattern its behavior based on its construction of God's nature, insofar as Christians tend to construct social reality based on their theology.

The social doctrine of the Trinity advocated by Jürgen Moltmann and others raises a vision of God-in-Trinity that is particularly suited to the development of an ethical response to colonizing discourse. Moltmann views the God revealed in Scripture as a Social Trinity, a fellowship characterized by non-hierarchical fellowship and reciprocal indwelling. Compared to traditional Trinitarian doctrines, this Social Trinity is "a more life-giving and liberating doctrine of God, more congenial to both feminist and postmodern sensitivities, closer to the biblical witness to Jesus, one with his Abba and the Spirit."[1] Instead of focusing merely on the inner life of God, the relationship among Father, Son, and Spirit, the doctrine of the Social Trinity is concerned with the manner in which all of creation is embraced within the divine fellowship. In particular, humanity finds its fulfillment only in relation to the divine fellowship. Conceived in this way, the Social Trinity is other-oriented. Trinitarian Persons are oriented to one another, and the love that defines the nature of the Persons circulates not only within the fellowship, but also beyond—it is directed to human others created in the image of the Trinity. Human love follows a similar pattern. It circulates within the human community and is simultaneously directed toward the divine Other. The social doctrine of the Trinity images God as non-hierarchical, relational, differentiated, and open to creation. As an archetype for human community, the Social Trinity is a liberating force. Instead of domination, separation, homogeneity, and closed systems, human community in the image of the Trinity is non-hierarchical, relational, differentiated, and open to creation. This is a theological perspective that rests on the hope of a God breaking into the "godforsaken present," shattering human illusions and hopelessness.[2] The self-emptying, kenotic love of God revealed through Jesus Christ promises forgiveness and leads to the possibility of reconciliation among human persons torn apart by discourses of power.

Self-giving, Trinitarian love provides both an archetype and a living space in which to engage in the process of decolonizing preaching. Christian preaching addresses a community that emerges from, participates in, and reaches toward the Triune God. The Trinity conceived as a social entity essentially deconstructs colonizing discourse, and thus reorients pulpit discourse toward a concrete and constructive vision of human life. This non-imperialistic theology encourages disengagement from destructive colonial/imperial behaviors and attitudes that distort genuine relationship with others, and redefines power in terms of love.

While this particular theological perspective is a fruitful conversation partner for postcolonial theory, it is an imperfect partner. There is

1. Wells, *The Christic Center*.
2. Bonzo, *Indwelling and the Forsaken Other*, 4.

no escaping the fact that social doctrines of the Trinity are Eurocentric, developed and debated within the Western academy. Social Trinitarian theology is in no way immune to the shaping pressures of imperialism. It is also a resolutely patriarchal theology, even as it makes room for alternative interpretations of God's nature as compared to traditional gender perspectives. For this reason, I have chosen to describe God as Creator rather than Father, despite the prevalence of paternal language in the literature.

Exploring the Social Trinity

Scripture testifies to humanity's experience with God in several guises and forms the basis for later theological constructions of Trinitarian fellowship. The Old Testament prophets revealed a God who chose to enter into the life of God's people and was wounded by their rejection and sinfulness. The New Testament "talks about God by proclaiming in narrative the relationships of the Father, the Son and the Spirit, which are relationships of fellowship and are open to the world."[3] Jesus is the revealer of the Trinity, and it is through Jesus' revelation that we come to understand God as Creator and parent. Jesus' baptism and call, proclamation, and ministry display a Trinitarian form—the events of Jesus' life take place through and in the Spirit and the presence of the Creator.

The suffering and death of Jesus Christ on the cross is at the very center of the life and nature of the Trinity. The cross is the summary form of God's history with us and for us.[4] Despite interpretations of the cross that lead to a triumphalistic view of Christianity, a Social Trinitarian understanding of the cross relates to humility, love-filled suffering, and the paradoxical power generated by the death of Jesus Christ. Moltmann describes the death of the Son as an *intra* Trinitarian event: "What happened on the cross was an event between God and God. It was a deep division in God himself, insofar as God abandoned God and contradicted himself, and at the same time a unity in God, insofar as God was at one with God and corresponded to himself."[5] Christ's incarnation, death, and resurrection altered the relationship between Son and Creator, suggesting that God is changeable, capable of suffering, and imperfect insofar as God is open to creation and willing to suffer pain for its redemption. Although God does

3. Moltmann, *The Trinity and the Kingdom*, 64.

4. Moltmann, *The Church in the Power of the Spirit*, 96.

5. Moltmann, *The Crucified God*, 244.

not suffer in the same manner as created beings, "he suffers from the love which is the superabundance and overflowing of his being. In so far he is 'pathetic.'"[6] God's suffering is an active form of suffering, a willingness to lay oneself open to another in passionate love.

It is only possible to characterize God as a suffering God if one employs Trinitarian terms. Specifically in relation to Christ's death, the suffering of the Creator was intimately bound up in the suffering of the Son. From a Social Trinitarian perspective, God longs for God's "other," divine and human, not out of some divine deficiency but because of a "creative fullness" that longs to put "creative love into action."[7] Thus, God's suffering is not an act of weakness but an act of creation. God's choice to exist in community, God's choice to live in relationship with creation itself—this openness to others leaves room also for suffering. God's passion in and through Jesus Christ, communicated by the Holy Spirit, is central to understanding the discourse of love among the Persons of the Trinity, the manner in which that love is directed toward creation, and the manner in which creation participates in Trinitarian love. God's capacity for suffering hints at both solidarity with a suffering humanity and a divine investment in the healing and recreation of human community. Rather than an inviolable, invulnerable God, it is the nature of the divine persons to suffer with and for others.

In order to highlight aspects of the Social Trinity that contribute specifically to the task at hand, I have identified four highly interrelated categories that characterize the nature of the Social Trinity. Freedom, mutual self-giving, self-differentiation, and openness are characteristic of the discourse of the Social Trinity, and provide a thought-provoking counterpoint to colonizing discourse as it occurs within human community.

Freedom

God the Creator is not distant or apathetic, but a suffering God who freely gives of self, making space within Godself for divine others (the Son and the Spirit) and human others. Moltmann understands God's freedom in the context of divine self-limitation. In effect, God chose to limit Godself so that there is space for creation to exist. Creation is preceded by the movement of God into Godself. This self-limitation or self-humiliation is an act of divine restriction that makes creation possible. In order to create heaven and

6. Moltmann, *The Trinity and the Kingdom*, 23.

7. Ibid., 45–46.

earth, God emptied Godself of all power and became like a servant—this is the self-emptying, kenotic love attributed to Jesus in Philippians 2:6–8.[8]

> Christ Jesus,
> who, though he was in the form of God,
> did not regard equality with God
> as something to be exploited,
> but emptied himself,
> taking the form of a slave,
> being born in human likeness.
> And being found in human form,
> he humbled himself
> and became obedient to the point of death—
> even death on a cross.

In this sense, the act of creation did not merely call life into being. The Creator also made a space within the divine community in which the creation itself could dwell. The Creator creates by withdrawing into himself and making space for creation. The incarnation of the Son is part of God's loving self-communication to the world, but also demonstrates God's self-limitation: "The divine kenosis which begins with the creation of the world reaches its perfected and completed form in the incarnation of the Son. By entering into a finite world, God limits himself, his omnipotence."[9] God is free to limit God's own omnipotence and free to enter into relationship with humanity.

Traditional interpretations of the Trinity envision a hierarchical structure, according to which God the Creator is an absolute subject and supreme ruler of a fixed hierarchy. Social Trinitarian theologians interpret God's revelation of the Trinity non-hierarchically. God the Creator, Jesus, and the Holy Spirit are united in such a way that divine rule is "exercised through the co-working of the Father, the Son, and the Holy Spirit."[10] Power is communal, an attribute shared by all three Persons, and the nature of the rule is "determined in and through the dynamic movement—the changing relations among the three Persons."[11] The almighty God is not an arche-

---

8. Moltmann, *God in Creation*, 88.

9. Moltmann, *The Trinity and the Kingdom*, 118.

10. McDougall, *Pilgrimage of Love*, 92.

11. Ibid., 81.

type of patriarchal power, but the parent of the crucified Son. God is not almighty power, but almighty and passionate love. God is defined through fellowship, not through power over property but "through personality and personal relationships."[12]

Jesus' life, death, and resurrection reveal God's kingdom as a place of love and liberation in which God is merciful: "there are no servants; there are only God's free children. In this kingdom what is required is not obedience and submission; it is love and free participation."[13] Love is the currency of divine fellowship—not unidirectional love that proceeds from the almighty God to Son, Spirit, and creation, but love that is given and received multidirectionally.

Through self-communication to divine and human others, God reveals God's own being. This revelation proceeds not out of any compulsion but because it gives God pleasure to reveal the truth of the divine nature. While some theologians such as Karl Barth have argued that God has no need of others, in the sense that God is love, God needs the world in order to be Godself. The God revealed in the Triune fellowship exhibits freedom in the friendship offered to humanity: through suffering, sacrifice, and by allowing men and women the opportunity to be free.

The Persons of the Trinity are free to love one another and creation. Freedom is found in and through a community of solidarity, not through oppression, dominance, and hierarchy. This is love that suffers freely on behalf of another and invites a free and joyful response from creation rather than a response formed in fear or because of subjugation. Such a vision of Trinitarian freedom does not support or justify human domination, nor hierarchical interhuman relationships. The discourse of the Social Trinity creates the possibility of freedom, equality, and solidarity. This does not imply that humans are equal to the Trinity; rather, the Persons of the Trinity are co-equal, and God has created humanity to live in communities of equality.

Mutual Self-Giving

God's very existence is located in community, as *Triunity*, or three-in-one. As discussed above, God is not a solitary, self-sufficient Lord who rules over Son, Spirit, and creation, but a Creator in need of both the divine and

12. Moltmann, *The Trinity and the Kingdom*, 198.
13. Ibid., 70.

created other. The Creator eternally loves the Son, who is a "like," but not an identical, divine being.

If God is to be understood *as* love, rather than simply one who loves, then God must be thought of as a Trinity, as a fellowship of love within Godself. Moltmann writes: "Love cannot be consummated by a single solitary subject," therefore, "if God is love he is at once the lover, the beloved and the love itself."[14] The Persons of the Trinity, while differentiated, dwell within one another. Here Moltmann borrows the ancient concept of *perichoresis*, "a movement from one to another, to reach round and go around, to surround, embrace, encompass."[15] The Persons of the Trinity move within one another, making space within for the others, making themselves inhabitable. The inner-Trinitarian perichoretic love reaches toward and around each Person of the Trinity, and flows out toward the human other, as ultimately evidenced by the incarnation and the cross.

The incarnate love of the Trinity literally dwelled within human community in the person of Jesus Christ. Not only has God taken up residence in the midst of the created order, but creation is drawn into the midst of the divine community. The relationship among the Trinity and creation is one of mutual indwelling. Creation is a part of the eternal love affair between the Creator, Son, and Spirit. It springs from the Father's love for the Son and is redeemed by the answering love of the Son for the Father. Creation exists because the eternal love communicates himself creatively to his Other. It exists because the eternal love seeks fellowship and desires response in freedom.

This divine love, or *agape*, overcomes any distance between God and creation, resulting in reciprocal relationships. Instead of a hierarchical relationship between God and creation, there exists a pattern of mutual love that corresponds to the love that exists within the Trinitarian community. This non-hierarchical view of divine-human mutual hospitality suggests that "the Creator finds space in the fellowship of creatures. The creatures find space in God. So creation also means that we are in God and God is in us."[16]

The Social Trinity continually crosses the boundary between itself and creation in an ongoing process of self-giving: "it is of the very nature of God's power to be in a constant state of donation, always turned out from

---

14. Ibid., 57.

15. Moltmann, *Experiences in Theology*, 316.

16. Moltmann, *Creation, Covenant and Glory*, 133.

itself, always giving and forgiving."[17] A vision of divine life characterized by mutuality and self-giving is in profound contrast to human systems that separate groups based on wealth, race, or other variables. While imperial philosophies seek the expansion and protection of the empire, human life in the image of the Trinity is more concerned with the preservation and protection of the other. Self-giving stands in deep opposition to the "take for oneself" motivating force of colonialism/imperialism.

Self-Differentiation

Traditional theologies have emphasized the unity of Creator, Son, and Spirit, simultaneously excluding the possibility that the divine persons possess differences from one another other than differences of power. Historically, it has been essential to emphasize the unity of the Trinity to protect monotheism. A Trinity can be easily mistaken for a collection of three gods, and indeed, Social Trinitarian theology has faced such criticism. It is possible, however, to conceive of the Trinity as a body in which the persons maintain essential unity without disintegrating into one another. Thus the importance of the term "three-in-one," Trinitarian terminology that stresses unity and difference at the same time.

This concept of triunity is based in Moltmann's identification of the activities of the Creator, Son, and Holy Spirit in the world. He highlights the distinct roles of the Persons of the Trinity in salvation history, roles that both reveal and constitute the being of the Trinity. For example, if the Son was sent by the Trinity to die on the cross (Romans 8:32; Galatians 2:20), then we must necessarily understand that the Triune God is differentiated, that there are multiple divine subjects who suffer in different ways according to the relationship of each to the other. The Persons of the Trinity exist in relationship, having divine nature in common; yet, their individual and particular natures are determined and defined only in relationship to one another. The divine Persons indwell one another, but they are not absorbed into one another, nor do they consist of one, homogenous substance. Personal distinctions remain, even as they indwell and participate within one another. Social Trinitarian theology images God as unity-in-diversity, "in eternity this process of self-differentiation and self-identification."[18] Here we return to perichoresis as an expression of this divine vitality and an eter-

---

17. Cunningham, *The Three Are One*, 144.

18. Moltmann, *The Trinity and the Kingdom*, 57.

nal life process that takes place in the Triune God through the exchange of energies. The Persons of the Trinity live in one another and dwell in one another. They are bound by a circulation of love. Perichoretic unity preserves plurality rather than erases it. Thus, unity emerges out of the particularity of the divine Persons, and personal differences remain. This aspect of God's life-in-Trinity challenges the homogenizing tendency of colonialism/imperialism. It asks us to ponder how human community can discover unity without erasing personal or group differences.

Openness

Instead of a static and fixed Trinity, the Social Trinity is characterized as a dynamic relational model,[19] according to which Persons of the Trinity are neither complete in themselves nor fixed in their identities. In perichoretic fashion, each Person is open to the other and makes space for the other. The Trinity opens to creation as the created other is drawn into fellowship. Each is affected by the other. Trinitarian love is not restricted to eternal circulation among the divine Persons. Moltmann writes: "The life of God within the Trinity cannot be conceived of as a closed circle—the symbol of perfection and self-sufficiency."[20] Instead, the Trinity sends the love of God into the world and is open to receiving the love of creation.

In Jesus Christ, the world was confronted with its tendency "to close itself down to the possibilities of the future."[21] Jesus Christ opened the way to a new present and future for humanity in the inner-life of the Trinity. The sending of the Son to suffer and die on behalf of the world was made possible because God exists in an open relationship to the world. The sending of the Spirit opens up the history of the Trinity to the history of the world. The future is not limited to what has happened before; indeed, the Spirit opens up the future in ways that are unimaginable and inconceivable.

Believers are integrated into Trinitarian history through the Spirit, in the experiences of baptism and fellowship, becoming participants "in the eschatological history of the new creation. Through the Spirit of the Son they also become at the same time participants in the Trinitarian history of God himself."[22] Salvation is the opening of the Trinity for the purposes of

19. Herrick, *Trinitarian Intelligibility*, 15.
20. Moltmann, *The Church in the Power of the Spirit*, 56.
21. Bonzo, *Indwelling the Forsaken Other*, 13.
22. Moltmann, *The Trinity and the Kingdom*, 90.

receiving and unifying the whole creation. According to Moltmann, "If one conceives of the Trinity as an event of love in the suffering and the death of Jesus—and that is something which faith must do—then the Trinity is no self-contained group in heaven, but an eschatological process open for men on earth [sic], which stems from the cross of Christ."[23]

The eschatological implication of this openness, this divine indwelling, is "the messianic hope for a future in which all of creation will be transfigured into the dwelling place of God."[24] The Trinity holds open the possibility of change and transformation in the present, and eschatological hope—not only a hope for another world, but for transformation for this world. Communities in *imago trinitatis* are incomplete. They are not self-enclosed nor self-sufficient units with fixed identities, but rather exist in relationship, are subject to change, and are open to God, to one another, and to all creation. This characteristic of the Social Trinity calls into question the tendency of empire to claim itself as the only viable alternative for human community. In the image of the Trinity, humanity is not locked into a fixed hierarchy, but instead is open to movement and alterations of power, all of which lead to the possibility of more equitable systems, as well as the possibility of freedom for those who have been held captive by inequitable systems.

Trinitarian Discourse as a Viable Alternative

The social doctrine of the Trinity casts a profound vision of God's inner being. The discourse of human community, within the Church and beyond, does not manage to produce even a pale reflection of Trinitarian discourse. The discourse of Creator, Son, and Holy Spirit, however, is a tantalizing possibility when compared to the destructive and self-serving discourses that have characterized colonial/imperial reality.

The question remains: does the Trinity provide an ethical norm for human community? Nicolas Federov once posited that "the Trinity is our social program," viewing the resurrection as an event that raised humanity to a new level of participation in the divine life that provides ethical imperatives for human relationships.[25] Others claim that a correspondence between Trinitarian community and human relationships is false or impos-

23. Moltmann, *The Crucified God*, 249.

24. McDougall, *Pilgrimage of Love*, 83.

25. Federov, *Le Christ dans la pensée Russe*, 404.

sible. Any comparison between divine and human relationship is necessarily limited, as creatures cannot possibly hope to copy God in any reliable way. Yet, as Volf argues, the very fact that we are created for relationship with the Triune God and in the image of the Triune God should lead us to seek a certain correspondence to God, albeit imperfect.[26] In his words, "Human beings are manifestly not divine. . . . Trinitarian concepts such as person, relation, or perichoresis can be applied to human community only in an analogous rather than a univocal sense. As creatures, human beings can correspond to the uncreated God only in a creaturely way."[27] An analogy comparing human and divine fellowships does not prescribe or perceive "a one-to-one correspondence between the patterns of fellowship that constitute the inner divine life with those that can be actualized within the human community,"[28] but is a flexible comparison or archetype. Moltmann writes: "Just as the three Persons of the Trinity are 'one' in a wholly unique way, so, similarly, human beings are the *imago Trinitatis* in their personal fellowship with one another."[29] Thus, the inner-Trinitarian community is an archetypal community that humans reflect only in part.

This correspondence between human and divine occurs within a messianic space, the already and not yet, recognizing that human likeness to God "is both an ever-present reality and an unrealized promise."[30] In the present, the Trinity is an active agent in the ongoing transformation of human community. Human nature is dynamic, existing in a state of transition between the now and not yet. This transition of humanity from forsaken to fulfilled depends upon God in Christ to bridge past and future, making possible a correspondence between God's life and ours. Humanity exists in a state of transition between *creatio originalis* and *creatio nova*, a process of *creatio continua*.[31] The Triune God is present in the church in the power of the Holy Spirit, and the Spirit continually acts to shape human community in the image of the Trinity. In the church, individuals together form the body of Christ, and it is through baptism that "believers are publicly set in Christ's fellowship; and through baptism in the name of the Triune God

26. Volf, "The Trinity is our Social Program," 404.

27. Ibid., 405.

28. McDougall, *Pilgrimage of Love*, 83.

29. Moltmann, *God in Creation*, 241.

30. McDougall, *Pilgrimage of Love*, 107.

31. See Moltmann, *The Trinity and the Kingdom*, 209; and *God in Creation*, 208–9.

they are thereby simultaneously set in the Trinitarian history of God."[32] To be set in the Trinitarian history of God is to participate in an integrative process of mutual indwelling (perichoresis), self-giving (kenosis), and self-differentiation.

Divine community and interdependence affect us as we are drawn into God's life and into the lives of one another and all of creation. Thus, human beings can be viewed as creatures whose fellowship is defined by mutuality and interdependence. Dietrich Bonhoeffer writes: "God's own life therefore provides a pattern for the life of his creation as an intricate community of reciprocal relationships,"[33] according to which all living things "live in one another and with one another, from one another and for one another."[34] The perichoretic love of the Trinity extends toward humanity, which is drawn into the very center of Trinity, into the space conceded by God. There arises the possibility of perichoretic, kenotic relationships among people, in which each is interrelated and love overflows from one human person to another.

Unlike the reciprocal indwelling of the Persons of the Trinity, perichoresis in the human community is vulnerable to discourses of power and sin. Human relationships are uncertain and unpredictable. Only eschatologically can humanity hope to transcend historical realities and enter into divine perfection. In the here and now, however, when humanity is drawn into this circular movement of the eternal divine love, the potential arises for human relationships characterized by mutuality, hospitality, and generosity. I understand perichoretic love to be the basis of both the unity and mission of the church. The unity of the Christian church is Trinitarian unity: "It *corresponds* to the indwelling of the Father in the Son, and of the Son in the Father. It *participates* in the divine Triunity, since the community of believers is not only fellowship with God but in God too."[35] This is the unity described in Jesus' prayer in John 17:20–22:

> I ask not only on behalf of these, but also on behalf of those who will believe in me through their word, that they may all be one. As you, Father, are in me and I am in you, may they also be in us, be one in us; so that the world may believe that you have sent me.

32. Moltmann, *The Church in the Power of the Spirit*, 266.

33. Bauckham, *The Theology of Jürgen Moltmann*, 185.

34. Moltmann, *God in Creation*, 17.

35. Moltmann, *The Trinity and the Kingdom*, 202. Emphasis original.

For Volf, the image of embrace captures the possibility of making space for the other within oneself. Although human beings cannot be internal to one another, cannot indwell one another in the same manner as Trinitarian Persons,[36] they can participate in an analogous process. Just like the open arms of Christ on the cross, "open arms are a sign that I have *created space* in myself for the other to come in and that I have made a movement out of myself so as to enter the space created by the other."[37] This process recalls God's self-contraction in order to make space for creation. Although humans do not in any sense create one another, they may need to restrict or limit their own self or freedom in order to allow for the other to be truly liberated. Such embrace depends on an attitude of equality and reciprocity, a willingness to recognize the other as other and as a person of value. Love that makes space for the other may be suffering love, requiring sacrifice of self or decentralizing oneself, so that "we can understand what it is to be them and what it is to be ourselves in their eyes."[38] The passion of Christ involves "self-giving love which overcomes human enmity and the creation of space in himself to receive estranged humanity. The same giving of the self and receiving of the other are the two essential moments in the internal life of the Trinity."[39] Christ's passion opens the possibility for humans to receive one another and overcome enmity. Self-giving does not involve loss of self. Rather, as the self gives something of itself, it limits itself in order to be expanded by the other. In Social Trinitarian terms, reciprocal relationships do not require homogeneity or the erasure of personal difference. Instead, individuality is recognized and given space, fostering a sense of unity in diversity.

Given the power imbalances inherent in colonial/imperial and postcolonial relationships, it is necessary to think carefully about what is reasonable for human persons in terms of giving and receiving. Those who have acted as oppressors are invited to give of self without expecting a reciprocal action on the part of the oppressed.

Any analogy between human relationships and divine relationships is strictly dependent on grace and God's prior self-giving. Humanity can only mirror Trinitarian life because God the Trinity has revealed itself. Humanity can only practice self-giving love because of gracious, Trinitarian

36. Volf, *After Our Likeness*, 213.

37. Volf, *Exclusion and Embrace*, 141.

38. Isasi-Diaz, "A New Mestizaje/Mulatez," 212.

39. Volf, *Exclusion and Embrace*, 127.

self-giving. Through the death and resurrection of Jesus Christ, we are set free to imagine and pursue human relationships that reflect the Triune God. As we are renewed, liberated, and transformed by God's actions, our estrangement from others "has been, is being, and shall be overcome."[40]

The Trinity is the source of the church's common life, and the image in which the church is created. Despite engagement with other, damaging discourses, God's children are continually drawn into the divine embrace, into Trinitarian discourse. The Trinity is the source, sustainer, and model for identity and relationships within the local and global church.

Deconstructing Colonizing Discourse

Colonizing discourse is inconsistent with the church in *imago trinitatis*. The discourse of the Social Trinity essentially deconstructs colonizing discourse, and reorients pulpit discourse toward freedom, self-giving, self-differentiation, and openness. This deconstruction points toward an alternative discourse for the practice of preaching that can replace existing colonizing discourse.

Deconstruction arises from a school of thought that views every interpretation and construction of the world as ambiguous and relative. It takes apart those constructions of the world and works toward reconstruction by replacing that which has been central with an alternative. In doing so, it questions the fixed hierarchies of power and meaning that are found within a text or discourse. Postcolonial criticism employs deconstruction insofar as it challenges the literary and cultural texts emerging from colonialism/imperialism and asks how they are enmeshed in colonial/imperial ideologies.[41] Deconstructing colonizing discourse is an essential task for decolonizing preaching, as it concerns our use of language and its effect on our relationships. Theologian Edward Farley describes how language affects our relationship to others: "In and through language, we render the other marginal, invisible, or such an absolute threat that anything we do to that other is justified."[42] Deconstruction makes space to ask questions from different angles, challenges assumptions, and opens up the field of inquiry to other voices, reminding us to listen more carefully for the whisper of the Triune God.

40. Hall, *The Cross in our Context*, 96.

41. Moore, "Postcolonialism," 183.

42. Farley, "Toward a New Paradigm for Preaching," 167.

Social Trinitarian theology locates human community in the space of the divine community. The social doctrine of the Trinity deconstructs colonialism/imperialism by "overturning and displacing"[43] the preferred terminologies of colonizing discourse such as hierarchy, separation, contempt for otherness, and fixedness with other terms consistent with God's life in Trinity: freedom, mutual self-giving, self-differentiation, and openness.[44]

Domination/Freedom

Colonizing discourse is a discourse of domination and oppression. Colonizers maintain moral, sexual, religious, and political control, often through violent means. The power of the dominant group is legitimated by an assumption of superiority that justifies the right of one group or nation to maintain power over another. The freedom of the dominant group to rule and retain control is perceived to be dependent on the limitation of subaltern freedom. The great irony is that colonizing discourse actually places both colonized and colonizer in a situation of captivity. The freedom of all is limited by the roles to which each is assigned. Thus, neither group is free to narrate their own histories or identities; they are held captive by the system itself.

Trinitarian discourse is a discourse of freedom. Creator, Son, and Holy Spirit exist as a non-hierarchal, power-sharing community defined by freedom, differentiated from one another. Human freedom is unceasingly desired by God. In the modern era, freedom has been defined as "lordship, power and possession."[45] The lord is free: all others are under domination, and therefore not free. God's liberty is revealed in friendship and love for humanity, not his lordship and power over humanity. Human community in the image of the Social Trinity desires to be free from domination and oppression, and desires the freedom of the others. In mirroring the love of the Trinity, humanity is truly free. It is no longer necessary to maintain strict hierarchies, nor allow one person or group to have dominion over another. Rather, each engages in self-limitation in order to expand the freedom of the other.

Trinitarian ethics, then, will result in a change in modern reason from "lordship to fellowship, from conquest to participation, from production

43. Derrida, "Signature Event Context," 329.

44. The social doctrine of the Trinity might also be fruitfully deconstructed according to various criteria, such as its Eurocentric bias, gender exclusivity, and, at times, a reinscribing of hierarchy.

45. Moltmann, *The Trinity and the Kingdom*, 56.

to receptivity."[46] Identity is not bestowed by those in power, but formed in relationship. A community shaped by the Social Trinity will define people "through their relations with one another and in their significance for one another, not in opposition to one another, in terms of power and possession."[47] Human identity is discovered as we are welcomed into the space of the Trinitarian fellowship.

Separation/Mutual Self-Giving

Colonizing discourse constructs oppositional relationships and maintains boundaries between the colonized and the colonizer, and between different races, genders, religions, classes, and castes. Boundaries are frequently maintained by violence, which has physical, psychological, and material consequences. The Triune God has overcome distances and boundaries between divine and human, between and among human communities. While colonial/imperial projects have guarded against hybridity in order to maintain cultural purity, the perichoretic nature of Trinitarian life accepts and welcomes hybridity and mixedness. Trinitarian love crosses artificial boundaries and leads to spaces of contact and encounter in which human beings are freed for mutual participation and fellowship. "As long as freedom means lordship, everything has to be separated, isolated, detached and distinguished, so that it can be dominated. But if freedom means community and fellowship, then we experience the uniting of everything that has hitherto been separated."[48] While colonizing discourse emphasizes opposition, Trinitarian discourse emphasizes connection, unity, mutuality, and hospitality. A relational, interpersonal understanding of God-in-Trinity contributes to a view of humanity that is relational and interdependent. Just as God is God only in relationship, so human beings are true human persons only in relation to God and to one another.

Separation among persons and communities precludes self-giving, as it is impossible to enter into reciprocal relationships, give of oneself, or enter into the suffering of another if strict boundaries are maintained. Self-giving in human fellowship is patterned after the life of Jesus in a spirit of inclusivity and generosity.

46. Ibid., 9.
47. Ibid., 198.
48. Ibid., 216.

Homogeneity/Self-Differentiation

Colonizing discourse is an essentializing rhetoric that overemphasizes differences among persons and groups in order to justify subjugation and divide and rule policies. Simultaneously, colonial discourse devalues otherness and seeks to suppress cultural difference. All cultures and races are compared to and perceived to fall short of the dominant group, which considers itself to be normative. Unity is enforced, and comes at the cost of social and cultural expressions of subaltern groups.

Trinitarian unity does not demand homogeneity but fosters a unity-in-diversity that values differences among individuals and groups. In order for love to proceed toward one's other, there must be personal distinctions between self and other. When the boundaries among persons are permeable, difference becomes basis for unity: "The very thing that divides them becomes that which binds them together."[49] God is both unity and multiplicity, and thus human unity and multiplicity are reflective of God's own nature. Christologically, *perichoresis* describes the interpenetration of the human and divine nature. Anthropologically, this means that others can exist within us and not consume or erase the self. There are boundaries that distinguish persons, but these boundaries are porous and fluid, and highly relevant for the production of meaning. In Moltmann's words, "We are who we are not because we are separate from the others who are next to us, but because we are *both* separate *and* connected, *both* distinct *and* related; the boundaries that mark our identities are both barriers and bridges."[50]

Fixedness/Openness

Colonizing discourse attempts to fix all reality according to the worldview of the dominant group. The language of the empire is considered normative, and all other voices are derivative. In addition, colonial/imperial systems are portrayed as a natural and permanent ordering of human life in a manner that shuts down the possibility of change. South African theologian Allen Boesak argues, "globally, we are confronted with an ideology that claims to be all powerful, without any alternative, and hence without any possibility of challenge or change."[51] When colonizers take up the

49. Ibid., 175.

50. Moltmann, *Experiences in Theology*, 66.

51. Boesak et al., *Dreaming a Different World*, 14.

mantle of oppressor, colonizing rhetoric claims that there is no alternative, no possibility for release, no hope of change or reconciliation between oppressors and the oppressed.

The discourse of the Social Trinity disputes the hegemony of empire. True love and power originate within the context of Trinity, and all other powers that claim totality are revealed to be idols. The empire's story is not the whole story, and there is room for the voice of the subjugated other. This discourse of hope opens the present to the possibility of the future, as God is continually reaching toward creation in order to recreate and transform the present. The Social Trinity has the potential to transform the nature of physical and emotional space: "In 'closed societies' space becomes the frontier that shuts in and shuts out. In 'open societies' the frontiers become permeable and turn into bridges of communication with others and with strangers."[52]

52. Moltmann, *The Coming of God*, 302.

4

Postcolonial Theory for Preachers

O PREACH IN A postcolonial ethos is to address a vast labyrinth of identities and histories. Preachers and listeners navigate complicated postcolonial realities every day, often without perceiving or naming these realities. The preceding chapters have begun to construct a new understanding of our postcolonial condition, in order to encourage preachers to rename and reimagine the nature of the space in which preaching occurs. An increasing awareness of the complexity of the colonial/imperial legacy brings with it a heightened need for a tolerance of ambiguity and overlapping categories. Preachers beginning to consider empire as a category of interest for contemporary preaching will benefit from the wisdom of those who have doggedly pursued the questions of postcolonialism. A vast and diverse body of postcolonial scholarship identifies and critiques colonial/imperial projects in history and the contemporary world. This collection of postcolonial theory will inform preachers as they seek to develop a broader understanding of the role of colonialism/imperialism in the world, the church, and the sermon itself.

Anticolonial sentiments have been expressed for as long as colonialism/imperialism has existed, but in the past century the field of postcolonial studies has taken a more definite shape as scholars and non-scholars alike have examined the interactions among colonizers and colonized persons, as well as exploring the characteristics of postcolonial spaces. The resulting literature is as complex as the problems it seeks to address. The average reader will not be enlightened by a glance at the inscrutable writings of the holy trinity of postcolonial scholarship: Gayatri Spivak, Homi Bhabha, and Edward Said. Nor is it possible for most readers or preachers to sift through ever-growing body of thought that continues to spring up in all regions of the globe. Postcolonial theory's conceptual vocabulary is itself a site of continual negotiation. Scholars from a range of social locations debate the meanings of key terms, resulting in ever-evolving and somewhat unstable definitions. Given the nature and purpose of postcolonial debate, it is unwise, if not impossible, to grant absolute authority to any particular or narrow definition. This multidimensionality allows for creativity and variety of opinion, yet it often results in prose that is almost incomprehensible. For that reason, the term "postcolonial theory" must be understood as a broad and plural category that encompasses multiple stances, perspectives, and commitments. Postcolonial theory in general is not particularly useful for busy preachers who do not have the time or the inclination to participate in what is essentially an endless debate, unless the theory is distilled and interpreted. Without denying the multitude of ideas and voices engaged in postcolonial debate, this chapter simplifies the theory and seeks to find a useful trail for North American preachers to follow through the mire. My intent is to allow preachers an easily digestible taste of the discipline and begin to imagine how its concepts might be applied to homiletic practice in North America.

Postcolonial theorists have developed some concepts and vocabulary that are particularly useful for pursuing a postcolonial perspective on preaching. Concepts such as hybridity and Third Space enable preachers to name the realities of empire and to more adequately comprehend the relationships among persons involved in the colonial/imperial process. Postcolonial criticism as a literary practice provides tools for reading historical texts, including the Bible, so that preachers may approach Scriptures from a perspective that honors colonial/imperial experience in the text and in the ecclesial space. Postcolonial biblical reading strategies deserve a chapter of their own, as biblical interpretation is so essential for the practice of preaching in many Christian traditions. As a sociological practice, postcolonial criticism aims its gaze at human actors caught in the web of empire as victims, bystanders, and perpetrators. Of particular interest here is the manner in which Christian theologians have joined in conversation with secular postcolonial theorists to explore the colonial/imperial and postcolonial situation of the church. Despite the challenges of postcolonial theory, it gives tremendous insight into the postcolonial situation and is a valuable partner for exploring the relationship between preaching and colonial/imperial reality.

What is Postcolonial Theory?

Postcolonial theory examines the manner in which histories and cultures of colonialism/imperialism intrude upon contemporary life. For example, it recognizes that many nations and groups within Africa, Asia, and Latin America are still treated as subordinate by European and North American nations. This subordination has resulted in significant economic, technological, and cultural inequalities that are further complicated by diaspora, race, class, and gender. Such inequalities extend across the globe, whenever individuals and groups hailing from previously colonized nations live within the bounds of nations associated with imperial power. Postcolonial theory asserts the right of all people to material and cultural well-being, and is "directed toward the active transformation of the present out of the clutches of the past."[1] In seeking to transform the present, postcolonial theory disputes Western hegemony and disrupts the discourse of the dominant by privileging the concerns of others who have been marginalized, oppressed, or silenced by the colonial/imperial process.[2] In effect, postcolonial theorists seek to recapture voices that have been lost or drowned out by the much louder and more powerful voices of those in power. Theorists assert that there has always been a counterpoint to the center. The margins of society created by colonial/imperial processes have continually produced meaning and responded to the center of power. These marginalized voices, however, have frequently lacked a platform or have actively been silenced by those who stand to gain from squashing opposition.

Postcolonial theory reflects to some extent a dialectical process among colonizers who seized power and colonized populations that have sought to regain independence and self-sovereignty.[3] Of course, the dialogue of postcolonial theory is not a binary exercise, not limited to colonizers and colonized persons, but extends to many others who find themselves occupying various location within imperial reality. For example, those who live in North America often find themselves in an ambiguous role vis-à-vis colonialism/imperialism. Both the United States and Canada are former colonies, now independent, although each nation achieved that independence in very different ways. Today, Canada and the United States are on friendly terms with their former colonizer, Great Britain. Yet the citizens

---

1. Young, *Postcolonialism: A Very Short Introduction*, 4.

2. Sugirtharajah, *Still at the Margins*, 12.

3. Young, *Postcolonialism: A Very Short Introduction*, 4.

of each nation are a highly diverse mix, and many have immigrated from colonized and formerly colonized nations. Both countries, although to different extents, hold power on the world stage, even as certain members of their own populations are powerless. Although the United States and Canada are productive locations for postcolonial dialogue, it is not a clear dialogue between oppressed and oppressor but a dialogue among many who have been affected in different ways by colonialism/imperialism.

Despite its origin in anticolonial struggles and resistance literature produced within the colonies themselves, postcolonial theory has largely developed within Anglophone universities by postcolonial subjects whose "origins and cultural affiliations lay elsewhere."[4] That is, much of the pioneering work of postcolonial studies has been accomplished within the West by scholars whose heritage lies in colonized regions. This, however, is beginning to change, and postcolonial dialogue is arising from outside the Western academy as other academics and non-academics are finding opportunities to contribute to the conversation.

Postcolonial theory draws from multiple sources, including literary theory, cultural anthropology, Marxism, sociology, feminism, and psychoanalysis. Scholars and others engage in a multifaceted conversation that arises from the dialectic among West and East, North and South, metropolis and periphery, and that ponders what happens when cultures are mixed together. The effects of such mixing are both positive and negative, and are an incontrovertible reality of life in the present day. This postcolonial conversation has consequences for both metropolis and colony, as both have been deeply, though differently, impacted by the colonial/imperial process, decolonization, and subsequent restructuring.

Challenging History

In the 1980s, literary scholars and cultural critics began rereading canonical English literature with an eye to the impact of empire on both the writing and subsequent interpretation of such literature. Inspired by the poststructuralist views of Jacques Derrida, Michael Foucault, and Jacques Lacan, scholars such as Gayatri Spivak and Homi K. Bhabha have affirmed, challenged, and expanded the pioneering work of Edward Said. These and other scholars contributed to the development of postcolonial criticism, an eclectic and cross-disciplinary perspective that investigates and exposes

4. Young, *Postcolonialism: An Historical Introduction*, 63–64.

"the link between knowledge and power in the textual production of the West."[5] Written texts shape the experience of both colonized and colonizer. Fictional narratives, religious texts, decrees, and laws can be used by colonizers to further inscribe colonial/imperial power. The written word can be used by the colonized to resist oppressive regimes or to tell another story that is absent from dominant portrayals of reality. Postcolonial interpreters use various tools and methods as an act of disobedience directed against the text and its interpretation, claiming that language itself needs to be decolonized, "to be remade in other images."[6]

Postcolonial criticism is applied not only as a reading strategy for texts but as a cultural practice. It is a category for exploring relationships and discourses between unequal partners. Such criticism searches history and contemporary relationships for written, spoken, and non-verbal discourses of power that stem from colonial/imperial processes. In both literary and cultural applications, postcolonial criticism analyzes the manner in which colonial/imperial representations have impacted, and continue to impact, the manner in which one group represents another. What does the dominant group say about a subordinated group? Is the portrayal positive or negative, accurate or self-serving? Throughout colonial/imperial history, subordinated groups have had little opportunity to speak for themselves publically. Thus, colonizers have been free to create and construct images of colonized persons. Postcolonial criticism seeks to make space for silenced voices, asking how the construction of knowledge is characterized by the absence of input from colonized subjects. Further, postcolonial criticism asks whether it is even possible for a colonizer to adequately represent the subaltern or colonized subject.

By attempting to undermine simple binary oppositions and contrastive ways of thinking, postcolonial criticism pays attention to the contact zones that arise between individuals and groups. What happens when colonizer and colonized come face to face, literally or metaphorically? What happens when different cultures and perspectives come into proximity? Generally, in these contact zones, predetermined categories and stereotypes are proven to be inaccurate. Contact zones are critical for preaching today. As I described in chapter 2, preachers and listeners find themselves in webs of relationships, often occupying multiple positions of power. It is the space between us—between preacher and listener, between listener and listener,

5. Sugirtharajah, *The Postcolonial Bible*, 93.
6. Rushdie, "The Empire Writes Back with a Vengeance," 8.

between the gathered community and the multitude of worlds beyond the church—it is that space that is both colonized and ripe for renewal.

The field of postcolonial theory has been dominated by literary scholars. However, in recent years, other fields have incorporated its insights, including history, economics, political theory, sociology, anthropology, and the arts. Robert Young notes the tendency of postcolonial theory to be a resolutely secular rather than spiritual discipline.[7] Even those postcolonial scholars hailing from locales embroiled in religious as well as colonial/imperial conflict, such as Franz Fanon from Algeria and Edward Said from Palestine, rarely considered the significance of religion for postcolonial inquiry.[8] In 2005, Kwok Pui-lan remarked that few of the insights gleaned from postcolonial literature had made their way into theological discourse.[9] Increasingly, however, scholars acknowledge the mutual significance of religion and postcolonialism. Theologians search for points of contact between Christian theology and postcolonial theory, recognizing that empire can no longer be ignored as a fruitful category for theological inquiry. In the words of Catherine Keller, there is no precolonial Christianity. The church was born into an imperial context and its first words were spoken in the languages of empire.[10] While some of us might argue vehemently that Jesus Christ sought to challenge and overturn prevailing empires, history has taught that the Christian church has been implicated in modern colonialism/imperialism by active choice, passive collusion, or pure accident. Theologians committed to a postcolonial perspective are anxious to overcome reluctance on the part of the church and the field of theology to acknowledge the profound relation between Christianity and empire.[11] Perhaps not surprisingly, postcolonial theory has made an impact on missional ecclesiologies as theologians reflect on the way Christian mission has interacted with colonialism/imperialism. Postcolonial criticism is beginning to find its way into Christian practice including worship, hymnody, and pastoral care. It is now time to bring it more fully into the field of homiletics.

---

7. Young, *Postcolonialism: An Historical Introduction*, 338.

8. Sugirtharajah, "Complacencies and Cul-de-sacs," 35.

9. Kwok, *Postcolonial Imagination and Feminist Theology*, 41.

10. Keller, "The Love of Postcolonialism," 222.

11. Ibid., 4.

Colonial Discourse Theory

Despite attempts on the part of colonizers to construct a one-way discourse, colonized persons have acted as initiators, agents, and respondents to the discourse of the colonizer. At the heart of colonial/imperial relationships is an ambiguity of power. While it appears that the colonizer is consistently more powerful, that power is continually undermined and called into question by colonized populations. In other words, neither power nor weakness are quite what they seem within colonial/imperial relationships. In the twentieth century, particularly in the aftermath of World War II and sweeping decolonization, came an extended reflection upon the past and present agency of the colonized within colonial discourse. The term "colonial discourse" refers to "the complex of signs and practices that organize social existence and social reproduction within colonial relationships."[12] Colonial discourse should not be confused with the related term "colonizing discourse," which I described earlier, and which refers specifically to one aspect of colonial discourse: that initiated by the more powerful group that seeks to dominate, separate, homogenize, and close systems. Colonial discourse, on the other hand, examines the entire discursive relationship that emerges between colonized and colonizer. The specific nature of such discourse varies according to time and place, but it is always embedded in other discourses such as patriarchy, poverty, and modernity. Colonial discourse, then, is not limited to topics such as land, identity, and race, but also addresses the manner in which colonialism/imperialism have interacted with issues of gender, economic stability, modern assumptions of science and progress, and many others. For example, colonialism/imperialism has had particular and unique consequences for women who are doubly marginalized in many cases—subordinated both by patriarchal systems within their own culture, and the colonial-patriarchal system. On the other hand, for some women colonialism/imperialism has been a source of relative freedom when compared to precolonial conditions in their region.

Colonial discourse theories, espoused by such scholars as Homi K. Bhabha, Edward Said, and Gayatri Spivak, recognize that colonial/imperial power has not been located solely in military and economic arenas but also within discourses of domination in which power and knowledge are inextricably linked. Colonizers' representations and modes of perception have been used as weapons of colonial/imperial power insofar as they have

12. Ashcroft et al., *Post-Colonial Studies*, 41.

sought to covertly colonize the minds and psyches of colonized subjects.[13] In symbolic and literal ways, colonizers have initiated one-way conversations in which the colonized other is inserted into the discursive space fully formed in the colonizer's own image. The success of colonial/imperial projects has relied, in part, on the ability of the colonizer to convince the colonized that the language of the empire is a natural and true order of life.[14] Postcolonial scholars challenge the ability of empire to impose a "language" or discourse, positing that the flow of power between colonized and colonizer is not unidirectional. Language and the production of knowledge are not closed systems: they are continually open to new meaning and negotiation. Systems claiming to encompass all known reality, including colonialism/imperialism, cannot account for the novelty, variety, and ambiguity at the heart of reality. According to various postcolonial theories, dominated peoples have continually sought to open up the systems of language and the production of meaning by contradicting or rejecting colonial/imperial constructions of subaltern identity and resisting the identity imposed by the colonizer.

The colonized are not simply the subjects or recipients of colonial discourse, but also agents who actively participate in the discourse by inserting their own voices in order to disrupt, resist, or accommodate the discourse of empire.[15] While Edward Said has tended to stress the agency of the colonizer and his or her role in oppressing the colonized other, Homi K. Bhabha has particularly stressed the active agency of the colonized, arguing that colonial power is not a straightforward form of oppression, but involves a complex interaction between the colonizer and the colonized that undermines any assumption of simple polarization. To suggest that power is entirely in the hands of the colonizer is an oversimplification. Colonial discourse is not a one-way flow of power from colonizer to colonized, but rather a complex interaction in which the identity of both colonized and colonizer are constructed. Thus, both colonized and colonizers shape and are shaped by this discourse.

Gayatri Spivak challenged the enlightenment assumption of autonomous agency over individual consciousness, claiming that human consciousness is derived from discourse. It is constructed, not chosen. In other words, we come to know who we are by what others say about us. The

---

13. Samuel, *A Postcolonial Reading*, 1.

14. McLeod, *Beginning Postcolonialism*, 19.

15. Samuel, *A Postcolonial Reading*, 3.

consciousness of subalterns is constructed by sources outside of self. The colonial subject is not free to be sovereign over his or her own construction of selfhood. According to Spivak, the colonial subject is defined by the voice of the colonizer.[16] The colonial/imperial process, then, constricts the freedom of colonized populations not only in physical and material ways, but also in highly personal subjective ways. In essence, colonialism/imperialism removes the right of colonized individuals and societies to define themselves. In this view, the representations of colonized subjects produced by the West completely overshadow the ability of the colonized subject to represent or speak for themselves. Western portrayals of subalterns are perceived by the rest of the world as more real and more accurate than subaltern self-portrayals. The suppression of self-portrayal is not the end of the story, however. Despite the manner in which colonial discourse defines or attempts to define the colonized, the subaltern or colonized subject talks back to the colonizer. Colonized persons may use the very tools of colonial power in order to "at least partially dismantle the colonizer's house."[17] For example, American critic Laura Donaldson suggests that teaching English in mission schools gave the colonized a common language, especially in regions with many local dialects and languages. By learning English, colonized peoples with different mother tongues were enabled to organize in various ways against the colonizer.

When the dialogical nature of colonial discourse is opened up, it becomes clear that colonial/imperial authority is not capable of completely destroying, naming, or portraying indigenous culture. The manner in which the colonizer represents colonized peoples is open to negotiation and transformation by colonized populations. The colonizer says "you are who I say you are," but the colonized subject refuses to be defined by the voice of the colonizer and asserts his or her own voice within the discourse. This undermines the authority of the colonizer by asserting the right of the colonized to narrate, or signify, his or her own experience. The voice of the other interrupts and calls into question the authority of the dominant.

Ambivalence, Hybridity, and Third Space

Ambivalence, hybridity, and Third Space are postcolonial concepts that are particularly useful for thinking about postcoloniality and preaching. These

16. Spivak, "Can the Subaltern Speak?"
17. Donaldson, "Postcolonialism and Bible Reading," 4.

concepts interrupt simple binary distinctions between colonized and colonizer, recognizing that reality and identity are somewhat ambiguous and have shifting meanings dependent on historical circumstance and personal interpretation.

"Ambivalence" is a term derived from psychoanalysis, and refers to a continual fluctuation between wanting one thing and its opposite, a simultaneous attraction toward and repulsion from a person, action, or object. According to advocates of colonial discourse theory, ambivalence is a hallmark of the complex relationship between the colonizer and colonized. "The colonial condition in all its power-laden inequality is a site crisscrossed with discourses of both affiliation to colonial power and resistance to that same power."[18] A colonized subject might despise the colonizer yet also desire to resemble the colonizer. For example, colonized persons might happily adopt the dress, language, food, or governing structures of their colonial masters, even as they adamantly dispute the right of the colonial master to rule over them. For the dominant colonizer, ambivalence is unwelcome because it disrupts the straightforward authority of the colonizer.[19] Colonizers desire compliant subjects who act according to the colonizer's expectations, but ambivalent colonized subjects tend to copy or mimic colonizers. Young gives a particularly interesting example of this phenomenon. The Roman Empire was a model for British imperialism; thus, the teaching of the Classics was an essential aspect of education in British schools and universities as a means of indoctrinating the ideology of empire. Young writes, "the English upper classes remained shamelessly in love with the culture of their own conquerors of over a thousand years earlier and imitated them in their own cultural productions and educational institutions. They were the first mimic men."[20]

The term "mimic men" refers to the postcolonial concept of mimicry, which describes the manner in which colonial subjects copy the language and behavior of their colonial masters either as a form of admiration or as a subversive tool. The example of teaching Roman ideology in British schools appears to represent an admiration on the part of the British of their former colonizers. Mimicry, however, can also undermine the authority of those in power. Colonized persons appear to be imitating their colonial masters, but they are doing so in a mocking, tongue-in-cheek kind of way. Bhabbha

18. Marshall, "Hybridity and Reading Romans 13," 169.
19. Ashcroft, *Key Concepts*, 13.
20. Young, *Colonial Desire*, 33.

called this "repetition with a difference." A recent cinematic version of the Lone Ranger is chock-full of examples of mimicry.[21] In this version, Tonto, the Lone Ranger's aboriginal side-kick, continually makes fun of the Lone Ranger's behavior and decisions. In what can only be described as a postcolonial retelling of a familiar story, the white man is portrayed as incompetent and silly. For example, when Tonto gets a first look at the Lone Ranger's iconic (and very tall) white Stetson cowboy hat, he asks "Couldn't you find a bigger one?" In making fun of the dominant character, Tonto acts subversively, calling into question the hierarchy of power that was explicit during the time and location in which the story is set.

Those in the margins talk back to the powerful center, unsettling the confidence and self-identity of those who occupy the central places of power. In the words of Robert Young, the periphery, which is classified by the center as "the borderline, the marginal, the unclassifiable, the doubtful," responds by constituting the center as an "equivocal, indefinite, indeterminate ambivalence."[22]

"Hybridity" is perhaps most familiar as an agricultural term. When one variety of plant is grafted onto another, the result is a new form of plant, a hybrid variety. In the automotive industry, a hybrid vehicle draws from multiple energy sources to fuel its movement. To draw an example from Christology, the central doctrine of the Christian faith rests on a human-divine hybrid in the person of Jesus Christ. The divine and human coexist simultaneously, different yet connected in essential ways.[23] Within postcolonial theory, "hybridity" refers to the mixedness of peoples and cultures. The practices of colonialism/imperialism have resulted in new cultures, as disparate groups have been brought together to occupy the same geographical location. In some cases, settlers from colonizing nations were sent to live within a foreign land, thus integrating to some extent with the original inhabitants. Settlements frequently resulted in intermarriage and children bearing the blood of two or more races or ethnicities, even as this was forbidden by some colonizing nations. Settlement also resulted in cultural fusions as aspects of two or more cultures were brought together.

In the more formal language of postcolonial theory, hybridity is "a strategic interruption of the manner in which cultural difference is constructed and sustained in colonial contexts."[24] The notion of cultural purity

---

21. Verbinski, *The Lone Ranger*, Walt Disney Pictures, 2013.

22. Young, *Colonial Desire*, 161.

23. Keller, *Divinity and Empire*, 68.

24. Abraham, "What does Mumbai have to do with Rome?" 382.

has been a sustaining foundation for colonialism/imperialism. The notion of hybridity challenges the existence of cultural purity by claiming that all cultures are changed and impacted by others. Thus, variety, difference, and mixedness are normative in all locales and the concept of pure race or culture is revealed to be a fallacy. In this sense, cultures are not discrete entities, but are interdependent and mutually constructed through continual interaction. Such a way of thinking undermines the binary oppositions that are so frequently used to distinguish among groups and persons, such as black/white, colonized/colonizer. According to this perspective, no identity or location is entirely fixed or independent. People and situations are continually shaped and reshaped by their interactions with others.

Boundaries are important locations according to postcolonial theory. Boundaries may be physical, such as a border crossing between two nations. They may be geographical, such as a line drawn on a map between two regions or nations that have distinctive populations and cultures. Boundaries may also be metaphorical, such as those perceived to exist between rich and poor, women and men, human and divine. Regardless of the type, boundaries are highly relevant places for encounters and the production of meaning. In the borderlands between cultures, regions, or peoples, it is possible to come face to face with others. These borderlands, or contact zones, are the breeding grounds of hybridity, as each group may be impacted and affected by others. Postcolonial hybridity assumes that boundaries are a location in which discourse occurs, and that boundaries are a site of negotiation. Boundaries between cultures or identities, then, are creative spaces in which identity and understanding may be challenged and negotiated. In colonial/imperial or postcolonial situations, the notion of hybridity challenges the construction and representation of both center and periphery by asserting that new transcultural forms arise in the contact zone.[25] Postcolonial theories of hybridity claim that whenever the cultures of colonized and colonizer come together, it will result in a new, hybrid culture. Neither group will remain the same. Hybridity is a subversive concept insofar as it claims that the colonizer does not ever succeed at fully integrating the colony into the dominant culture.

In itself, hybridity is neither a positive or a negative consequence of empire. It is simply what happens when people and ideas move from one location to another. The consequences of hybridity, however, are significant. Encounters in the borderlands are not easy or straightforward, and one

25. Ashcroft, *Key Concepts*, 114.

should not imagine that encounters involve a handshake. Borders, boundaries, spaces of hybridity are also locations of conflict and hostility, of fear, of confusion. Cultures will be changed by one another, just as persons entering into conversation will take and receive from one another. Yet change comes at a cost. While some cultures may easily adapt to one another, for others it is an agonistic process involving tension, anger, even war.

Bhabha employs the spatial metaphor *Third Space* to describe the location in which new cultures are produced, the space in which persons and cultures come together. This liminal space between cultures opens up the possibility of cultural hybridity that entertains difference without an assumed or imposed hierarchy. In this sense the in-between Third Space is a space of intervention and creativity.[26] In the Third Space, the whole notion of culture is brought into question, and it is possible to recreate relationship based on an entirely new set of rules that are not defined by history or common assumptions. In the Third Space, identities and relationships are negotiated. This hybrid strategy or discourse opens up "a Third Space of negotiation where power is unequal, but its articulation may be equivocal."[27] Agency may be available to the colonial subject or subaltern who would otherwise be ignored or silenced. However, this space does not automatically equalize power relations. Some individuals or groups are doubly or triply marginalized. It is a space of "dislocation and displacement"[28] in which colonial discourse is decentered and the discourse of the dominant is called into question, challenged, interrupted by the voice of the subaltern. The power of the colonizer is contested as the colonial subject challenges the unitariness of dominant discourses, revealing them to be fractured, unstable, and plagued by ambivalence.

Bhabha's theory casts a positive vision for social change, and hybridity and Third Space appear to be liberating categories. However, the exact nature of the social change for which Bhabha is calling remains elusive. While the Third Space is a powerful image for imagining social encounters and the destabilization of colonial/imperial power, it is not clear who may enter this space and under what conditions. Why do some encounters result in new, stronger relationships while other encounters result in violence and destruction, or the entrenchment of irreconcilable difference? Although hybridity does not resolve the tension between cultures, it does signify a

---

26. Samuel, *A Postcolonial Reading*, 30.

27. Bhabha, "Cultures In Between," 208.

28. Bhabha, *The Location of Culture*, 163.

creative space that protests notions of purity and recognizes the power of difference for generating meaning. As he explains, "in its dominant form, it is claimed that [hybridity] can provide a way out of binary thinking, allow the inscription of the agency of the subaltern, and even permit a restructuring and destabilizing of power."[29] In the Third Space lies the possibility of reinscribing and resignifying the past, which might result in new authority structures and political initiatives. According to Bhabha, this space has the potential to free us from the seemingly inevitable repetition of history, what he calls "repetition without a difference."[30] In other words, encounters in the Third Space provide an opportunity to interrupt the ongoing tension among cultures or groups, which is simply repeated from generation to generation without ever being considered or examined.

The dislocation, or decentering, of the power of empire may be of tremendous help for preaching in the midst of empire. In many ways, empire is an omnipotent reality that has claimed the allegiance of all. North American Christians participate in empire in myriad ways, including our participation in the modern industrial complex. If preachers desire to respond to empire, they must do so in full awareness that they themselves stand within the imperial complex. It is difficult to critique from within. However, within the Third Space suggested by postcolonial theory, those held captive by empire can find a voice to challenge the unitary claims of empire. It is a space to point out the failures and gaps of imperial power, to reveal the empire as a fraud in comparison to the Triune God. In the postcolonial Third Space, we become agents with voices that can claim alternatives in order to promote change. This concept will be explored more fully in chapter 7.

Cautionary Tales

A postcolonial perspective holds tremendous promise for opening a discursive space between colonized and colonizers, between past and present, between the hegemonic West and the developing world, but it is necessary to proceed with caution. Postcolonial theorists and practitioners critique colonial/imperial structures, but they also critique postcolonial theory itself. Postcolonial scholars have frequently criticized their own discipline, resulting in a continual evolution of both theory and practice. Scholar

29. Bhabha, quoted in Prabhu, *Hybridity*, 1.
30. Bhabha, "Cultures In Between," 167–214.

Anne McClintock, for example, has rightly argued that the term "postcolonial" is prematurely celebratory, especially for those who find themselves in Northern Ireland, the West Bank, East Timor, and other occupied territories.[31] Decolonization does not guarantee the end of colonial/imperial subjugation, as imperial power may continue in a variety of ways, including its adoption by indigenous governments.

Postcolonial theory, unlike anticolonial resistance, has emerged largely from a privileged, academic position, and it is has been controlled by Western scholarship, prompting Seamus Deane to suggest that "postcolonial discourse emerges as a ruse of power, a contemporary form of Western liberalism, radical in its openness to otherness but Western in its gaze on otherness."[32] In this sense, postcolonial perspectives emerge as a neocolonial attempt by the empire to assign a role to former colonies, in which the empire "commands them once again to speak its language."[33] When applied transhistorically, postcolonial criticism risks conflating important differences between colonized peoples, treating them as a collective unit rather than acknowledging their vast diversity. The situation for colonial subjects differed according to factors such as time period, geographical location, culture, religion, and the goals of the colonizers. Postcolonial feminists are quick to point out that the experience of colonized women was different than that of men. In addition, the experience of women varied drastically depending on when and where they lived.

These cautions and critiques must be taken seriously. Postcolonial inquiry itself must be continually decentered and deconstructed, and informed by a variety of global voices. Despite its limitations, postcolonial theory offers a unique window into the past and present realities of both colonized and colonizing peoples. When undertaken with an awareness of its potential dangers, it is possible to mitigate some of the concerns raised above. The ideas presented above contribute to the task of decolonizing preaching.

31. McClintock, "The Angels of Progress," 253–66.

32. Deane, "Imperialism/Nationalism," 356. Young argues, however, that some of the foundations of postcolonial theory, such as poststructuralism, were first theorized in non-Western cultures (*Postcolonialism: A Very Short Introduction*, 67–68).

33. Sugirtharajah, *The Postcolonial Bible*, 111.

PART III

A Toolbox for Decolonizing Preaching

5

Preaching with a Postcolonial Imagination

CONTEMPORARY PREACHERS ARE FULLY aware that the world is broken. Relationships within the Christian community, the relationship between God and humanity, relationships among global citizens—all seem to fall short of what God-in-Trinity has desired and imagined. Poverty, war, natural disaster, illness, inequality, economic uncertainty, and environmental ruin are all important issues to be addressed in sermons. The continuing presence of colonizing discourse is one concern among many, even as colonialism/imperialism are deeply, even causally, related to many of the troubles afflicting the human community. To preach from a postcolonial perspective is not to ignore the other ailments of a diseased world, but to name colonialism/imperialism as an ongoing reality and a cause for concern in this time and place. This kind of preaching does not attempt to offer easy answers, nor can it untangle the complex threads that compose the fabric of postcolonial life. What this kind of preaching can do is imagine and proclaim a new structuring of human relationship that is more reflective of God's own life and God's desire for the beloved creation.

Biblical scholar and theologian Kwok Pui-Lan defines "postcolonial imagination" as "a desire, a determination, and a process of disengagement with the whole colonial syndrome which takes many forms and guises."[1] Preachers, listeners, sermons, the homiletic academy—all are vulnerable to both the lure of empire and colonizing discourse. Preaching with a postco-

1. Kwok, *Postcolonial Imagination and Feminist Theology*, 3.

89

lonial imagination involves a desire to disengage from empire, to disrupt and reorient colonizing discourse toward a more life-giving discourse. It recognizes that the world is not as it should be, and begins to construct a new way of interpreting both past and present. To decolonize preaching is to imagine a human community shaped by discourses of love and freedom, rather than dominance and captivity. Such preaching aims at the transformation of an unjust and oppressive world. In the words of homiletician Christine Smith, preaching is "nothing less than the bold, fearful, interpretation of our present world, and an eschatological invitation to a profoundly different, new world."[2]

Strategies for Decolonizing Preaching

A toolbox of postcolonial homiletic strategies will assist preachers as they respond to colonizing discourse as it occurs in the church, the sermon, and within the broader context of everyday life. The strategies below are uniquely designed or adapted for addressing colonizing discourse. It is important to note, however, that liberation preaching and African American preaching have long confronted issues of power, privilege, wealth, and race, issues integrally related to postcoloniality. Thus, a vast homiletic literature already exists that is not labeled postcolonial, yet provides considerable resources for decolonizing preaching. The Black and Hispanic churches are well ahead of others in terms of reflection on these issues, and they are already intimately acquainted with the effects of empire, especially with regard to race and economic status. Preachers in Canada and the United States will benefit from familiarity with both the theology and homiletic methods of liberation preaching and African American preaching. While it is impossible to do justice to the wisdom and insight offered by scholars and pastors who have long practiced preaching within those traditions, I want to acknowledge the significance of their work for postcolonial preaching.

The lure of empire is so persistent, the consequences of colonialism/imperialism so widespread, that it is difficult to imagine a few strategies will make any difference at all. These strategies are small footsteps along a grand highway. Sermons are always small steps on a much greater journey. Preaching forms and molds congregational identity week by week, idea by

2. Smith, "Preaching."

idea, text by text. Each of the strategies described here is a contribution toward the shaping of the communal postcolonial imagination.

Naming Colonizing Discourse

Decolonizing preaching begins with the personal practices of the preacher. Preachers are invited to search their own sermons, culture, experience, and relationships for colonizing discourse. A postcolonial homiletic "asks preachers to honestly critique their traditions, naming ways Christianity and Judaism have participated in the oppression of some of their own people, and to honestly state what must be resisted and changed about the traditions to make them more just."[3] Within the fellowship of the local and global church, as well as in their own ministries, preachers will uncover evidence of power imbalance, inequality, domination, the devaluation of otherness, as well as those ways in which Christians close their minds and hearts to hope and possibility for change.

Naming colonizing discourse aloud in sermons is a highly sensitive endeavor, especially for preachers and listeners who benefit from imperial systems such as global consumer markets. Christians are often reluctant to admit the failings of the historical church, which makes it particularly difficult to name the ways in which the church itself has been implicated in colonialism/imperialism. Quite rightly, contemporary church folk have tremendous admiration for past generations of Christians, especially those who have forged new pathways as missionaries. They will be reluctant to criticize the methods and outcomes of the past. Some will desire to affirm the centrality of Christian doctrine as compared to global indigenous faith or other religions, approving of the church's historical cooperation with the colonial/imperial system.

This kind of naming will not be easily spoken or easily received. Yet preachers speak on behalf of not only those who have perpetrated colonizing discourse but also those who have been victims. "Remaining silent in the face of our acknowledged complicity is not an option for a Church such as ours who professes Jesus Christ as Lord of our time and our history."[4] There are times when this will mean that preachers "confess that Christianity is

---

3. Smith, *Preaching Justice*, 2.
4. United Church of Canada, "Living in the Midst of Empire," 26.

deeply implicated in the violence of the world,"[5] and name out loud the complicity of the church in the imperial process.

Preachers need not condemn the church of the past, but confess that it is a fallible institution that makes mistakes even as it seeks to be faithful. Colonizing discourse can be categorized as destructive according to a number of moral or ethical perspectives. Christians, however, answer to the ethical imperatives of the Triune God, which are patently opposed to colonizing discourse. Preachers can hold up historical and contemporary examples of colonizing discourse and ask whether or not they are consistent with our understanding of God's nature and God's hopes for human community. The church is not, and never has been a perfect reflection of God's life-in-Trinity.

Most preachers will struggle with naming colonizing discourse as it occurs in the ongoing relational dynamics of a particular congregation. One does not want to stand up in the pulpit and announce that one group within the church is colonizing another. Preachers can encourage introspection, name an alternative ordering of Christian relationships (already present in Scripture and in theology), and ask questions about issues of race and power, wondering aloud whether and how these matter in the life of "our congregation."

Sermons should name empire as an aspect of the broader context in which contemporary Christians live and serve. The "principalities and powers" named by Paul continue to shape the experience of Christians (see, for example, Ephesians 6:12). Responding to those powers is an unavoidable action for the church today. Possible responses include accommodation, denial, active resistance, or ambivalence. In the postcolonial context, sermons expose the principalities and powers, including colonizing discourse. Thus, listeners are enabled to make more conscious and thoughtful choices about the manner in which they will respond.

An example arises from the issue of religious diversity. I am often surprised by the level of anti-Muslim rhetoric uncritically circulated within Christian circles, including jokes sent by email, or throwaway comments that reveal a lack of cultural understanding. The cultural and religious prejudice of this kind of colonizing discourse does not appear to be intentional, but rather completely unexamined. Preachers, perhaps, can remind listeners to reflect carefully about what they say out loud or electronically forward to others. By naming it as colonizing discourse, sermons might

5. Lischer, *The End of Words*, 146.

interrupt the unreflective practices of listeners. Naming and describing colonizing discourse will also assist listeners to reflect more deeply on world events, perhaps recognizing some of the colonial/imperial roots of issues such as ongoing land claims made by Native Americans, the global expansion of the mission field, or trouble in the Middle East.

The public naming of colonizing discourse is not intended to spark self-hatred or unhealthy guilt in preachers and listeners. As a communal act, preaching addresses all who have been implicated in the systems of empires—perpetrators, victims, and bystanders. Naming the truth can be liberating, especially for those who perceive themselves to be victims of colonizing discourse. It is also liberating for those who recognize their own participation in colonial/imperial projects at the expense of others and for those who find themselves held captive to empire. In naming the strands of colonizing discourse that weave through ecclesial and public relationships, preachers loosen the grip of empire, paving the way for another vision of reality shaped by an image of God rather than an image of earthly power and control. A theological naming of imperial reality will lead to the imagining of a new future governed by freedom, mutuality, variety, and endless possibility.

Engaging Difference and Diversity

Most congregations are characterized by some degree of difference and diversity, although this variety might not be immediately visible. Even in monocultural congregations, there exist various experiences and personal histories. Preachers should develop a sense of the diversity and cultural difference characterizing the nation, neighborhood, and congregation. This will involve not only studying demographic information and engaging in conversation with those within and beyond the congregation, but also brushing up on local, national, and global history and current events.

Exegeting the listening community will aid preachers in gaining an understanding of how different individuals and groups have been affected by the colonial/imperial process.[6] Globalization is a contemporary outgrowth of colonialism/imperialism, and it has radically altered the meaning of *local*. In the words of homiletician Eunjoo Mary Kim, "It is not realistic to assume that the congregational culture is static or limited to its locality."[7]

6. Tisdale, *Preaching as Local Theology.*
7. Kim, *Preaching in an Age of Globalization,* 9.

Listeners will likely dwell at the center of a web of relationships that transcend the immediate neighborhood, even stretching across the globe.

As noted in chapter 2, Leonora Tubbs Tisdale encourages preachers to take on the role of ethnographer in order to gain an understanding of the unique subculture of a congregation. A congregation may include more than one subculture. Each congregational subculture may relate to the congregation in a different manner, as well as experience various kinds of relationship with the cultures beyond the congregation. A word of caution to preachers attempting to navigate these complexities in the role of ethnographer: Kathryn Tanner notes that the term "ethnographer" implies a superior perspective, which was central to modern practices of anthropology and "one of its major goals was to aid the administration of colonized people as manageable wholes."[8] A preacher acting as ethnographer should be careful not to assume his or her perspective is superior to those being observed.

As preachers consider the specific culture and subculture of their listeners, they will be better able to gauge the possible effects of their words upon listeners. Listeners will hear sermons according to their own context, expectations and assumptions. A particular listener may hear, interpret, and respond to a sermon according to their personal experience vis-à-vis empire. A preacher might ask, for example, "what historical memories, what colonizing discourses are spoken or unspoken in a worship service in which a white preacher stands up to speak to a congregation composed of Caribbean, Guyanese, African, and Indian congregants?" A First Nations listener may hear a sermon based on the exodus narrative differently than a non-aboriginal listener. A black listener of South African origin might hear a sermon on racial reconciliation differently than a white listener of South African origin. Some listeners may respond positively to a sermon that challenges the notion of empire, while others will be offended, perhaps because they themselves benefit so conspicuously from the spoils of empire.

Taking into account the variety of colonial/imperial and neocolonial experiences present in congregations, especially in an age of diaspora, preachers can predict and prepare for the proliferation of meaning derived from their words by a diverse congregation. This is a limited possibility, of course, as we cannot know the totality of "the effects our speech generates."[9] Some knowledge of listeners' imperial experience at least raises the poten-

8. Tanner, *Theories of Culture*, 43.
9. Alcoff, "The Problem of Speaking for Others," 17.

tial that preachers can predict some of the possible or probable effects of a sermon on listeners.

Preachers will benefit from an awareness of their own social location, especially as it compares to the social locations of listeners. Christine Smith argues that "all preachers should be able to not only describe their social location, but also articulate significant ways in which their social location influences their biblical hermeneutics, their theological thinking, their pastoral sensitivities, and their homiletical methodologies."[10] She perceives that preachers from marginalized ethnic or cultural communities are usually better able to articulate social location than Canadians or Americans of European descent, who experience privileges because of their class and ethnicity. For this group, it is an act of justice to name and articulate one's social location and "to take responsibility for the limited, prejudicial, and often oppressive dimensions of one's human identity in relation to the rest of humanity."[11]

Cautious Representation

In her book *Imperial Eyes,* Mary Louise Pratt reflects on the practice of travel writing in the eighteenth century, and how books by Europeans about non-Europeans constructed subjects in the minds of a reader.[12] Back home, readers were influenced by the colorful descriptions of the colonies and their inhabitants provided by travel writers. Thus, they came to imagine colonial subjects in a particular manner. Preachers also create and produce others in the minds of their listeners, although in a manner different from world travelers of the eighteenth century. The proliferation of media today means that listeners and preachers come to the worship space with preconceived notions about others from news reports, movies, and other sources. Thus, the preacher produces subjects in conjunction with a variety of other sources, including the personal experiences of listeners as they have encountered others in their own lives. The preacher may confirm, dispute, or create an alternative subject in the minds of listeners.

When I returned from travelling in India, I wanted to describe what I had seen, and "introduce" the people whom I encountered on the way. My portrayal of the tribal Christians of central India, however, was

10. Smith, *Preaching Justice*, 2.

11. Ibid., 3.

12. Pratt, *Imperial Eyes.*

unintentionally perpetuating a stereotype of poor, helpless, uneducated persons entirely dependent on the guidance and benevolence of Canadian churches. I was "creating" these subjects in the mind of my listeners. In that case, I was likely the sole source of information for listeners, as most had not come across visual or literary images of India's tribal people. I was also inadvertently constructing myself and my listeners as central, and the Indian Christians as peripheral. The dissonance between my representation and the reality I encountered in India led me to reconsider the words I chose to speak about my Indian friends.

Sermons often allude to the lives of others and tell the stories of others. Is it possible for preachers to accurately represent others? In what manner can we talk about the experiences and identities of others? From a postcolonial perspective, preachers must carefully consider representations, descriptions, and characterizations about the identity and perspectives of others. A postcolonial homiletic seeks to honor the real situations and identities of others and problematize the process by which preachers create subjects by paying attention to the social location of self and others, by listening to the voices of others, and by the way others contradict our perceptions and representations. We can only speak on behalf of others if we are already in conversation with them, which involves learning from and listening to others.[13]

Preachers cannot escape the problem of representing others, yet can strive to be as accurate as possible and clear that whenever we speak about others in our sermons we speak out of our own biases and limited knowledge. Our perceptions of others are always inaccurate to a certain extent. Our representations of the needs, experiences, and identities of others are not definitive or complete but are open to correction and contradiction. What we know or think we know about others might be affected by an inadvertent sense of cultural superiority. For those of us living in Canada and the United States, a sense of cultural superiority has likely been cultivated since we were small children. It is necessary then to advocate a posture of humility and self-awareness as we approach such conversations with others in the local congregation or the global arena. In the modern imperial era, colonized persons were viewed and described according to the Western gaze, which attributed various characteristics to colonized others, often untruthfully, in order to protect the interests of the empire. Colonial/imperial powers insert their own story into the story of others: "Anglo-European

---

13. Rose, *Sharing the Word*, 111.

colonialism defined, changed, and re-defined the cultural identity of colonized people."[14] The preacher's witness or testimony can question the authority of the Western gaze and break the silence about oppression and injustice, contradicting the myth that one group contains and controls the "whole truth."

Sermons can also draw attention to misrepresentations or inaccurate depictions of others within the broader culture and media. Shawn Copeland has asked to what extent might sermons be a vehicle to address, complicate, or correct social representations of others in the media.[15] By challenging or correcting widely held assumptions about others, preachers contest the dominant construction of reality, thereby encouraging listeners to call into question prevailing stereotypes and assumptions that distort authentic relationship and Christian love.

Assessing Power Dynamics

Power inequalities stemming from colonial/imperial systems complicate preaching at multiple levels. Some congregations, or some members of congregations, benefit from the structures of empire that oppress others, and "may actively or passively participate in maintaining systems of oppression."[16] As Western churches themselves are increasingly marginalized, congregations may desire to retain or maximize the power available to them by strengthening relationships with economic or business systems that seem successful. To complicate matters further, even as churches in Canada and the United States lose power in their own locations, they continue to possess significant power relative to their global brothers and sisters. Despite the church's discourse of loss and recent experience of exile within North America, most white, mainline preachers are still closer to the center of power than to the margins. Thus, many preachers hold power relative to certain members of their congregation and global churches, even as they struggle with the loss of pastoral authority within and beyond the church.

At the same time, powerful Christians in Canada and the United States are held captive by colonizing discourse, principalities and powers,

14. Jiménez, "Toward a Postcolonial Homiletic," 161.
15. Copeland, "Body, Representation and Black Religious Discourse."
16. Allen, *Preaching and the Other*, 76.

and other oppressive systems.[17] All are negatively affected by colonizing discourse. In different ways, all are held captive by oppressive systems and need to be liberated. Preachers occupying positions of power are called to recognize the need for liberating gospel in their own lives, not to live out the experience of the oppressed other but rather to discover "in what ways he is oppressed, and learn about how the same system which oppresses others also oppresses the seemingly powerful."[18] The presence of power inequalities and multiple oppressions in local and global spaces signals a need to come to terms with one's own relative power. For preachers, this means taking into account the power inequalities existing between preacher and congregation, among congregants in a given church, and between local and global churches. As preachers recognize these power inequalities, they may be seized by a desire to repent of the ways in which they unintentionally wield power over others.

North American congregations may consist of immigrants with a national experience of colonization, as well as individuals or groups that belong to formerly colonizing nations. The rhetoric of colonialism/imperialism aims to convince the colonized persons of their inferiority and the superiority of the colonizers. This sense of inferiority may be internalized, which creates a power imbalance around the table and within the pews, even as we strive for equality. Listeners with an internalized sense of inferiority may overvalue the authority of the preacher and ignore or suppress their own theological insight.

Preachers will benefit from an extended reflection upon power dynamics and inequalities. Several questions may be particularly helpful in guiding this reflection: How am I held captive by empire? What power dynamics are present in the congregation by virtue of gender, race, economics, colonial/imperial experience? How is power used by others within the congregation? How do various listeners perceive my authority? How does my knowledge of my subject matter, my knowledge of listeners function as a weapon of power? How can I foster a sense of wonder that allows me to participate in the lives of listeners, increasing my own vulnerability as I make space for their knowledge and experience?

17. Campbell, *The Word before the Powers*.

18. González, *Liberation Preaching*, 26.

Decentering Perspectives

Postmodernity refutes the modern assumption of common, universal experience. Individuals and groups experience and interpret the world in different ways according to their social location and the particularity of their life experience. Modern assumptions about the universality of thought and perspective have led to a belief that the preacher could speak confidently for others, that one voice from the pulpit could address the needs and perspectives of everyone, everywhere. Preachers addressing a contemporary postcolonial context must contend with a multiplicity of perspectives and recognize they cannot speak for all.

Preachers may choose to simply acknowledge the limitations of their own experience, publically recognizing that theirs is but one voice among many. This is accomplished in part by incorporating a conscious *I* into the sermon: simply incorporating such phrases as "I believe," "from my perspective," and "according to my own experience," just to name a few.

Another possibility is to actively seek to include more voices and perspectives in the preaching process: during sermon preparation, within the sermon itself, and after the sermon has been delivered. Gandhi once said that "three-fourths of the miseries and misunderstandings in the world will disappear, if we step into the shoes of our adversaries and understand their standpoint."[19] This is true not only for adversaries but also for the multiplicity of others who we encounter, those local and global Christians with whom we engage in both imaginative and literal ways. By participating in conversations and representing conversations in sermons, preachers "begin the slow, often tedious process of learning the presumptions, conventions and idioms needed to make the others' views intelligible." This process involves "both a willingness to listen to differences and a willingness to hear those differences in their fullness."[20] A postcolonial hermeneutic for preaching prompts preachers to gather input from a variety of written and human sources in sermon development. To interact with a variety of voices and perspectives will lead not only to a better understanding of the power dynamics described above but also to richer and more robust biblical, theological, and social interpretation. Liberation theologies, for example, claim God is located most fully at the margins and invite those at the center to become students of those who dwell at the margins. In the colonial/imperial

---

19. Gandhi, *Collected Works*, 26:271.
20. Fowl, *Engaging Scripture*, 157.

context, the West has assumed not only that it has special access to truths about God, but also that God has ordained and blessed the hegemonic center. Dominant Western theological interpretations have pushed aside any marginal interpretations. A necessary correction occurs when the margins are allowed to talk back to the center—effectively decentering the location of theological discourse. For both preachers and listeners, conversation with others "involves remaining open to the idea that there are things we do not and will not know, and to the likelihood that we will not even know that we don't know them."[21] Insights gained from these encounters enable more faithful interpretation of Scripture, as well as nurturing the relationships among Christians near and far.

In practical terms, how might these encounters take place? Preachers can choose to engage in broader theological discourse. An increase in global publishing and the countless resources available on the Internet mean that preachers need not rely solely on commentaries and lectionary resources emerging from the West. Reading sermons by preachers from other geographical and social locations helps us better understand the context of other Christians and gain a sense of how those communities interpret scriptural texts for preaching. What if we occasionally sent a sermon overseas for comment? Or engaged in online Bible study with other preachers? Preachers can learn a great deal from listeners and other preachers who have experienced, suffered, or observed the consequences of colonizing discourse firsthand.

In the course of daily ministry, preachers have many opportunities to encounter others in meaningful ways. Pastoral visiting is an ongoing task for many clergy and is an opportunity for preachers to learn about the colonial/imperial history of families and to discuss whether and how that history still affects them and their relationship with others. Bible studies, roundtable lectionary study groups, as well as congregational and community social events allow preachers to gather information about how listeners are affected by colonial/imperial diversity within the congregation, and how they perceive others in the global church and beyond. These encounters are opportunities to gain feedback about sermons and test the preacher's perceptions against those of listeners.

It is possible for both preachers and listeners to have face to face encounters with global others through world travel. Facebook and other social media offer an unprecedented opportunity to connect, instantly, with

---

21. Gringell, "The Absence of Seaming," 108.

Christians all over the world, including other preachers. Even in poor regions with unstable electrical systems, mobile technology is often readily accessible and inexpensive. I visited a small church in my travels through central India. We shared a meal on the veranda, in the dark, because the church did not have electricity. I was surprised to be invited to befriend that congregation on Facebook! Social media has proliferated even in underdeveloped regions of the world. Language can be a barrier, but one of the enduring consequences of British imperialism is that English continues to be spoken in many nations. This is a positive consequence of empire insofar as English-speaking preachers in the West are able to engage in deeper relationships with global others.

As an imaginative exercise, preachers might find it useful to test their spoken words and insights against the presence of real and imagined others. To do this exercise, stand in the pulpit in an empty worship space. Picture the congregation, reflect on its diversity, its needs. Now imagine that there are visitors: perhaps a local Imam, a young man from Ghana attending a local university, a cousin of a church member visiting from Mexico. Now, as you reflect on the sermon you are preparing, ask yourself "Can I say this? Is this true? How will this thought or sentence be heard or experienced by those who hear?" Catherine and Justo González offer a good example of what it means to take into account the experience of listeners: "In a Thanksgiving service, for instance, we must be ready to repeat in the presence of our Native American sisters and brothers whatever is said about the ownership of the land."[22]

In local and global conversations, not all voices are heard equally. The voices of some will be louder, and some will feel safer speaking up than others. A postcolonial perspective will caution that conversations should be approached in full awareness of power differentials. Although descriptions such as "multi-vocal" or "pluriphonic" are frequently used to describe preaching models and methods that involve conversation with others, "it should be pointed out that in our postcolonial world, all the voices are not equal and some cultures dominate center stage, with the power to push the rest to the periphery."[23]

Justo González notes that a growing number of people are coming to reject the self-image imposed on them by colonizers. The colonized, who have believed what they have been told about themselves by their

22. González and González, "The Larger Context," 31.

23. Kwok, *Postcolonial Imagination*, 42.

oppressors, now want to define themselves. This process has led to the demise of empires and continues among those who have been colonized.[24] Our conversations with others near or far will be affected by history and by present misunderstandings, stereotypes, and half-truths. Others might perceive us as implicated in their oppression as collaborators of colonial/imperial power because of our skin color or ethnicity. We may harbor suspicions or stereotypes about others. On all sides, then, there are barriers that might prevent or problematize our willingness to enter conversation.

Negotiation and Contradiction

In the sermon itself, preachers act as facilitators, bringing listeners into proximity with others far and near. Engagement with others during sermon preparation and in the course of continuing education provides access to stories and images for sermons that bring distant others into imaginative proximity. This engagement comes about not only through the kinds of conversation discussed in the previous section, face-to-face contact, but also through an intentional reading of newspapers, blogs, and literature as discussed below.

Conversations allow preachers and listeners to hear God's word as it emerges from others, providing an important corrective or reference point for assumptions of preachers and listeners and the representation of these assumptions in sermons. The sermon itself can be expanded by the inclusion of contextual voices, sharing the stories of those who have been alienated, silenced, or ignored—preferably in their own words. A single sermon might even offer contradictory perspectives, further opening up the internal dialogue of the listener and the communal conversation of the congregation. Postcolonial theory views negotiation as an important process within colonial discourse. The sermon itself can reflect a kind of negotiation. Walter Brueggemann uses the language of testimony-countertestimony to describe the truth-seeking of the Old Testament. One story is challenged by another, allowing a fuller portrait of truth to emerge. He states, "countertestimony can break the silence of oppression which is enforced by the establishment, and contest dominant 'truths' through an appeal to openness and hope."[25] Two contrasting perspectives in one

24. González, *Liberation Preaching*, 12.

25. For this and other insights, I am indebted to a presentation by Walter Brueggemann at the Homiletics and Biblical Studies panel discussion on "Testimony and the

sermon, for example, engage a process that is essentially a negotiation of truth. The preacher might say something like "Here's what I see, but, here is how another person sees it . . ." In this case, the preacher's testimony is challenged by the counter-testimony of others.

There are limits to our ability to fully know others, let alone speak for others, and it is possible to leave a space within the preaching task for others to challenge the constructions of the center and define themselves. Leaving room for counter-testimony and the negotiation of truth both acknowledges the limits of the preacher's and listeners' grasp of truth and paves the way for a much broader perception of God's action in the world. Practical considerations mean that in our sermons subalterns can rarely speak for themselves in a literal way.[26] On a metaphorical level, the sermon can be open to counter-testimonies that supplement or challenge the always partial truths of the preacher. Sermons can also include the specific words and reports of others, delivered by the preacher or another voice.

Fictional Encounters

Art and literature are eloquent sources for coming to terms with the postcolonial condition. Creative endeavors have been a means by which colonized and marginalized people have been able to respond to empire. Art can be subversive, can allow a path for the marginalized to represent themselves in a manner not wholly comprehensible to others, and can be a tool for resistance or communication. The stories told in the music, visual art, dramatic art, screen art, and literary fiction produced by colonial and postcolonial subjects open up postcolonial discourse: "Stories are at the heart of what explorers and novelists say about strange regions of the world; they also become the method colonized people use to assert their own identity and the existence of their own history."[27] In a reversal of the one-way, top-down flow of colonizing discourse, relatively powerful preachers become students of less powerful others as they explore the art produced by those who occupy the space of postcoloniality.[28]

Personal" at the Society of Biblical Literature Meeting, Atlanta, GA. (November 2010). Unpublished paper entitled "The Risk of Testimony."

26. See Spivak, "Can the Gendered Subaltern Speak," and also Jiménez, "Toward a Postcolonial Homiletic," 167.

27. Said, *Culture and Imperialism*, xii.

28. See González, *Liberation Preaching*, 27.

Works of literary fiction can assist preachers to expand their postcolonial imaginations and gain broader insight into the realities and legacies of colonialism/imperialism. When we read literature written by the other, we are challenged to enlarge the stories by which we live. Novels written by authors from all colonial and postcolonial contexts are widely available. Of course, novels reflect the experience of the author and often the experience of the author's community, but are limited in their ability to represent whole cultures. However, by reading novels and sharing excerpts in sermons, preachers can gain insight into particular social locations through the words of others. For example, diasporic authors such as Jhumpa Lahiri offer insight into the lived experience of hybridity that is very common in urban settings. Lahiri has written collections of short stories, as well as a novel entitled *The Namesake* that details the life of a second generation immigrant whose parents are Bengali and now live in Boston. Others offer insight into the destructiveness of colonizing discourse. A fine example is Barbara Kingsolver's *The Poisonwood Bible*. Kingsolver describes the experience of an American pastor and his family as they serve as missionaries in the Belgian Congo. She traces the changing perceptions of the colonized inhabitants of the Congo through the eyes of the four daughters of the pastor.

A novel by an American medical doctor, Abraham Verghese, *Cutting for Stone*, tells the story of twin boys born to an Indian nun and British doctor in Ethiopia, a story in which the main characters themselves serve as an illustration of hybridity. Verghese creates a vivid portrait of the experience of those at the receiving end of Western benevolence. Imagine a sermon about global mission or development that incorporates the story of an American doctor who visits the Ethiopian mission hospital. Dr. Harris encounters a huge stack of Bibles in a variety of languages; the matron identifies these Bibles as gifts from Western churches. "We need medicine and food. But we get Bibles." Matron smiled. "I always wondered if the good people who send us Bibles really think that hookworm and hunger are healed by Scripture? Our patients are illiterate." The Bible storeroom is labeled Operating Theatre 1. She goes on to explain that donors have sent money for another operating theatre, when what the hospital really needs are medical supplies. So the matron buys the supplies, and names the broom closet Operating Theatre 2.[29]

In conversation, Mr. Harris learns there is a disconnect between the actual needs of these Ethiopian people and the manner in which generous

---

29. Vergese, *Cutting for Stone*, 189.

Westerners perceive those needs. Included in a sermon, this fictional conversation might illustrate the necessity of being in conversation with others, especially those whom we desire to help. This kind of conversation might thwart a tendency to paternalistic benevolence. Sharing this story in a sermon offers food for thought about the actual needs of global others in a nonconfrontational manner.

Resistance and Critique

Empire and colonizing discourse are negative influences that shape our lives, often without our knowledge or consent. While the naming of both the presence of empire and colonizing discourse is essential, it is not necessarily enough. Preachers may also choose to engage in active resistance against these forces. In his book *The Word Before the Powers: An Ethic of Preaching*, homiletician Charles L. Campbell envisions preaching itself as nonviolent resistance to the domination of the world by principalities and powers. The purpose of proclamation, in keeping with Jesus' own resistance to the powers, is to continue this shaping of the Christian community into a community of resistance. The church is then free "to live faithfully in the face of the powers of death."[30] Campbell argues that preaching itself has colluded with these powers of death, participating "in acts and systems of domination that involve harmful forms of psychological, spiritual, and physical coercion that must be considered violent . . . at a subtler level, preachers have often used language in ways that support and sustain the Domination System."[31]

Preachers are invited not only to cease participation in colonizing discourse but also to actively resist. This is nonviolent resistance, unlike some of the methods employed historically by anticolonial movements and advocated by colonial critics such as Franz Fanon. The Word of God, as it is present in preaching, resists and defeats colonizing discourse not by sword but by a healing word that emerges in the space between postcolonial subjects.

Shawn M. Copeland, in an article about the role of preaching in resisting the popular and highly objectionable portrayal of black women's bodies, suggests sermons invite the gathered community to "question, analyze, transform their social and historical situation." The sermon, as it arises

30. Campbell, *The Word before the Powers*, 188.
31. Ibid., 83.

from within a particular history and tradition, seeks to "give back to the community its own history, its cultural memory, its creative potential, its soul."[32] By reminding the listening community of its own identity, rooted in the Triune God, the preacher proclaims God is always stronger than any earthly system or empire. Insisting on the loving power of the living God is a subversive, even treasonous statement when uttered in the midst of empire. To draw on the central image of the Christian faith, the proclamation of the cross is in essence a subversive statement. Rome made the ultimate attempt to suppress the opposition they perceived arising from Jesus and his disciples. The cross is representative of the Roman Empire's power. Jesus died on that cross but he did not remain dead. The power of Rome was revealed as folly, impotent against the power of God to bring life out of death.

An aspect of resisting empire is to critique the policy and actions of governments and other powerful institutions insofar as they exhibit imperial perspectives and enable colonizing discourse. A sermon by Jeremiah Wright identifies imperial projects of the United States, as well as Israel and South Africa, in a manner that must have been shocking to many listeners, especially as it was preached a few days after September 11, 2001. This sermon is an extreme example of naming and would likely be inappropriate in most pastoral contexts. Yet it effectively retells American history from the point of view of those whose lives have been negatively affected by US imperialism:

> We took this country by terror away from the Sioux, the Apache, the Iroquois, the Comanche, the Arapaho, the Navajo. We took Africans from their country to build our way of ease and kept them enslaved and living in fear. Terrorism. We bombed Grenada and killed innocent civilians, babies, non-military personnel; we bombed the black civilian community of Panama, with stealth bombers, and killed unarmed teenagers and toddlers, pregnant mothers and hard-working fathers. We bombed Qadaffi's home and killed his child. Blessed are they who bash your children's heads against the rocks. We bombed Iraq. . . . We've bombed Hiroshima, we've bombed Nagasaki, we've nuked far more than the thousands in New York and the Pentagon and never batted an eye. Kids playing in the playground, mothers picking up children after school, civilians, not soldiers, people just trying to make it day by day. We have supported state terrorism against the Palestinians, and black South Africans, and now we are indignant.

32. Copeland, "Body, Representation and Black Religious Discourse," 192.

Because the stuff we have done overseas is now brought into our own front yard.[33]

A postcolonial imagination will lead preachers to retell history with an eye to what has been ignored or suppressed, inserting the history of those whose story has not been told. Rather than relying on the rhetoric of empire, preachers will be suspicious of predominant explanations and reports. They will seek to interpret events through the much broader lens of Christian theology.

Beyond the Sermon

A few years ago, I attended a worship service in an urban congregation. The guest preacher proclaimed a strong message about peace from the perspective of process theology. It was clear that her message was slightly beyond the comfort zone of the congregation, but she used the opportunity to plant some new seeds and raise some interesting questions. Immediately following this sermon advocating peace among Christians and throughout the earth, the choir stood to offer an anthem. Their choice: "The Battle Hymn of the Republic." It is difficult to imagine a more inappropriate musical follow up to that particular sermon. This example reminds us the sermon does not stand alone. The practice of preaching generally takes place within the space of Christian worship. Preachers often have responsibility for shaping other aspects of the worship service. All of what I have said about the sermon can be applied to other liturgical acts. Worship leaders should search all liturgical materials, including prayer and hymns, for signs of implicit or explicit colonizing discourse. While the preacher might not have a great deal of influence over the design of the worship space itself, it is useful to be aware of some of the signs and symbols of empire that invade the worship space. These include national flags and war memorials.

Conclusion

The process of decolonizing preaching is a painful and difficult one for both preachers and listeners. I have named some of the pitfalls and specific challenges. Decolonization will not happen overnight and will require a great

---

33. Wright, "The Day of Jerusalem's Fall." This sermon was delivered at United Trinity Church.

deal of trial and error. Patience, prayer, and continual theological reflection are essential for preachers and the gathered community.

What Walter Brueggemann says about testimony can be applied to postcolonial preaching:

> It is an utterance that is playful, open, teasing, inviting, and capable of voicing the kind of unsure tentativeness and ambiguity that exiles must always entertain, if they are to maintain freedom of imagination outside of the hegemony. Such utterances do not yield flat certitudes that can be everywhere counted upon. Rather they yield generative possibilities of something not known or available until this moment of utterance, so that new truth comes as a telling, compelling surprise.[34]

As much as I have tried to offer concrete strategies, postcolonial preaching is a homiletic perspective that must remain open and flexible, accepting ambiguity and contradiction. Unlike the modern assumption that all truth is accessible and all can be discovered through rigorous scientific method, postmoderns acknowledge that truth is at times elusive, that certainty is unattainable. We cannot ever fully know divine or human others. The other remains somewhat a mystery, and it is important to honor that mystery. Rather than try to tame or demystify otherness, we can leave room in the process of preaching for the mysterious presence of human and divine others. This space of mystery is a hope-filled space. We may not understand how God is working, but we believe God alone can overcome the barriers of colonizing discourse. The Triune God has the freedom to do a new thing beyond our imagining.

34. Ibid.

6

Rereading Scripture: Postcolonial Biblical Interpretation

URING A VISIT TO Peru, Pope John Paul II met with representatives of a Peruvian indigenous movement who said to him:

> John Paul II, we, Andean and American Indians, have decided
> to take advantage of your visit to return to you your Bible, since
> in five centuries it has not given us love, peace or justice. Please,
> take back your Bible and give it back to our oppressors, because
> they need its moral teachings more than we do. Ever since the
> arrival of Christopher Columbus a culture, a language, religion
> and values which belong to Europe have been imposed on Latin
> America by force.
>
> The Bible came to us as part of the imposed colonial transfor-
> mation. It was an ideological weapon of this colonial assault. The
> Spanish sword which attacked and murdered the bodies of the In-
> dians at night became the cross which attacked the Indian soul.[1]

This striking indictment of the Christian church points to the manner in
which the Bible has been used as a weapon of colonial/imperial power. The
Bible has been part and parcel of the colonial/imperial process, arriving in
the hands of Western colonizers and often used to justify their presence in
foreign lands. The biblical texts were disseminated by the church but also
formed the basis of normative Western values that have been thrust upon
colonized populations.

The Bible has also been a source of positive and redemptive transformation for colonized persons who perceive it as an ally against colonial/

1. See Richard, "1492," 31.

imperial power. Some have recognized the liberating message of Scripture and subsequently adopted and adapted the Christian faith as an affirmation of freedom, equality, and personhood, and as a tool to subvert colonial/imperial authority. Liberation theologians from a variety of ideological standpoints, including feminist, Latin American, Dalit, and African American, have found within Scripture a vision for freedom and an impetus for both resisting oppressors and building more just systems. The relationship between the Bible and colonialism/imperialism is complex. It is remarkable that the very same Bible has justified colonizing discourse and contradicted it at the same time, depending on whose interpretation, where, and when.

Preachers engage biblical texts on a weekly basis, and biblical interpretation is an essential aspect of the preaching process. Postcolonial preaching is biblically centered. Scripture is a key source of revelation—it communicates the identity of Creator, Son, and Spirit, and thus it helps us understand our own identities in relation to the divine. If preachers are to address a community that dwells in the midst of empire and has been impacted by colonialism/imperialism, it is necessary to reflect carefully on the hermeneutical process. Postcolonial biblical interpretation considers the manner in which the Bible has been implicated in the colonial/imperial process, and also how it speaks a word of liberation into a postcolonial ethos. It looks for a plurality of voices within the text itself and listens for a plurality of interpretive voices in the church and beyond. This chapter explores the topic of postcolonial biblical interpretation as it has emerged from postcolonial theory, setting the stage for a practical and abridged postcolonial biblical hermeneutic suitable for weekly sermon preparation. A postcolonial hermeneutic is a key tool for decolonizing preaching.

The Bible and Colonialism/Imperialism

Most of the texts contained in the Bible reflect the various colonial/imperial contexts of the day. Jeremiah Wright explains, "In biblical history, there's not one word written in the Bible between Genesis and Revelation that was not written under one of six different kinds of oppression, Egyptian oppression, Assyrian oppression, Persian oppression, Greek oppression, Roman oppression, Babylonian oppression. The Roman oppression is the period in which Jesus is born."[2] The early Israelites shuffled between their

2. Wright, "Reverend Wright at the National Press Club."

homeland and the mighty empire of Egypt, where they were captive slaves. Their greatest moment is God's action in leading them out of empire, across the Red Sea, and into their own land. The narratives of the Old Testament, the voices of the prophets, the gospels, and the epistles—all reflect the experiences of people under imperial captivity or threatened by the ruthless power of empire. The Israelites and the Jewish people are not the only ones whose captivity is encapsulated in biblical texts. Some, like the Canaanites, were victims of Israel's own colonial/imperial project.

It is a great irony that "Christianity, born as a movement of colonized people, could also come to mimic the empire."[3] Biblical texts were shaped by their original imperial contexts, and they have in turn shaped other imperial contexts. Even as the Exodus, the incarnation, the death, and resurrection of Jesus Christ all point to liberation from the powers of empire, the Bible has become associated with empire and employed as a tool in the oppression and subjugation of various populations. The Bible—sacred and beloved—is unsafe and problematic insofar as the biblical texts, as much as any other work of literature, encapsulate the interests and agendas of those who have produced and interpreted them.[4] Feminist scholar Elisabeth Schüssler Fiorenza claims "it is not only the intentions of the 'original authors' that must be considered, but also the manner in which texts and interpretations of texts have functioned in historical and political settings."[5] Biblical interpretation is not a neutral task. The agendas and contexts of the interpreter will affect the manner in which the text is understood and acted upon. Textual interpretation has serious ethical and political consequences.

As the central text of the Christian faith, the Bible has been upheld as a normative text, and countless communities have shaped their identities based on it. Communities whose values differed from normative interpretations of biblical values have been judged to be in need of correction, or civilizing. In his classic text *Orientalism*, Edward Said outlines the role of the eighteenth-century revolution in biblical studies in representing the "Orient" and constructing representations of others.[6] Biblical texts have been used as warrants for colonial/imperial expansion, thus reinforcing the idea that churches in "Asia and Africa have been recipients of the gospel

---

3. Keller et al., *Postcolonial Theologies*, 29.
4. Sugirtharajah, *Postcolonial Criticism and Biblical Interpretation*, 100.
5. Fiorenza, *Rhetoric and Ethic*, 28.
6. Said, *Orientalism*, 17.

as a gift from the benevolent West to enlighten the heathen."[7] Franz Fanon has argued that the religion of the colonizer (Christianity) can colonize the minds of colonized peoples, paralyzing them against responding to or resisting the oppressive rule of the colonizer because of its emphasis on meekness and forgiveness.[8]

Closer to home, biblical interpretations have contributed to immeasurable physical and cultural violence against Native North Americans by justifying the conquest of land and the spread of civilizing mission. Laura Donaldson, referring to Christian denominations' apologies to Native North Americans for historical treatment says "the inadequacy of these responses foregrounds the need for a critical paradigm that would enable churches to confront their histories in a more direct manner."[9] Postcolonial biblical interpretation is a critical paradigm that desires a more just and faithful framework for interpreting Scripture in the midst of the complex relationship between Bible and empire.

Introducing Postcolonial Biblical Interpretation

Postcolonial biblical interpretation takes seriously the reality of empires in the ancient and contemporary worlds and explores "the enigma of how a disparate set of texts written in the margins of the Roman Empire, if not from its underside, eventually became, collectively, the charter documents of a post-Constantinian, which is to say, imperial Christianity."[10]

This interpretive style is highly attuned to the social locations of the authors and interpreters of the biblical texts. Sugirtharajah categorizes it as a "mental attitude rather than a method."[11] A postcolonial approach to biblical studies recognizes the diversity of colonial/imperial and postcolonial experience, and advocates for conflicting voices within the text itself and within the interpretive community. Postcolonial criticism does not seek to recover a single meaning of the text, but recognizes "a multiplicity of meanings."[12] It does not collapse or homogenize various interpretations, but reads contrapuntally; that is, approaches the text with a simultaneous

7. Sugirtharajah, *The Postcolonial Bible*, 105.

8. Fanon, *The Wretched of the Earth*, 93.

9. Donaldson, "Postcolonialism and Bible Reading," 2.

10. Moore, *Empire and Apocalypse*, 122.

11. Sugirtharajah, *The Postcolonial Bible*, 93.

12. Sugirtharajah, "From Orientalist to Postcolonial," 24.

awareness of multiple perspectives, including colonized and colonizer, metropolis and periphery, and others.[13] In Said's words, to read contrapuntally is to employ a strategy "modelled not . . . on a symphony, but rather on an atonal ensemble."[14] In the biblical text, there are voices from the center and the periphery, voices of domination, submission, resistance, and collaboration—but these voices are not always distinct. Donaldson argues that interpreters should approach texts with a "multiaxial frame of reference" that considers not only gender, culture, and class, but "the intersection of anti-Judaism, sexism, and cultural and religious imperialism in the history of the text's interpretation."[15]

By examining and exposing threads of colonial/imperial domination embodied in biblical texts and subsequent interpretations of those texts, postcolonial biblical interpreters search for "alternative hermeneutics while thus overturning and dismantling colonial perspectives."[16] These alternative hermeneutics will bring to the forefront marginal aspects of texts, and aim to recover and reassert the identities, cultures, and traditions that "colonial Christianity has marginalized, erased, suppressed or pronounced 'idolatrous,'"[17] while recognizing the text itself may already be engaged in this process of recovery and reassertion. The text is respected as a resource that potentially "enables ordinary poor and marginalised people to interpret the biblical text in a manner that foregrounds and emphasizes their own lived experience and contextual realities."[18] Western academic practitioners of postcolonial biblical interpretation have much to learn from the experience of their social, cultural, and economic others. This involves a responsibility to "ensure that the yearnings of the poor take precedence over the interests of the affluent; that the emancipation of the subjugated has primacy over the freedom of the powerful; and that the participation of the marginalised takes priority over the perpetuation of a system which systematically excludes them."[19]

By remembering and acknowledging past and present colonial/imperial projects, postcolonial interpreters can provide a new ground for

13. Said, *Culture and Imperialism*, 318.

14. Ibid.

15. Donaldson, *Postcolonialism and Bible Reading*, 8.

16. Sugirtharajah, *The Postcolonial Bible*, 16.

17. Moore, *Empire and Apocaplyse*, 15.

18. Reddie, *Mark and its Subalterns*, xi.

19. Sugirtharajah, *The Postcolonial Bible*, 113.

interaction among parties separated by power inequalities, such as those who gather for worship in American and Canadian churches. A post-colonial interpreter will interrogate the biblical text at particular points, especially where it shows signs of "ambivalence, incoherence, and self-sub-version—and not least where its message of emancipation subtly mutates into oppression."[20] The interpreter learns to see the imprint of colonialism/imperialism in the text itself, and becomes aware of the danger of "colluding with textual tactics and interpretations that might reinforce a politics of dominance."[21] In awareness of his or her responsibility to honor the voice and experience of the marginalized, the preacher must decide whether to "applaud and collude with the text, or resist its stance."[22]

A Fresh Lens for Familiar Texts

Biblical scholars have adopted postcolonial reading strategies for a growing number of texts across the biblical canon. In order to introduce preachers to a few of the interpretive stances made possible within postcolonial interpretive frameworks, I have chosen an Old Testament and Gospel text and described a particular postcolonial interpretation. This leads into a more in-depth study of the Gospel of Mark and the story of Jesus and the Syrophoenician Woman.

Reading as a Canaanite: The Exodus Narrative

> The Lord said, "I have indeed seen the misery of my people in Egypt. . . . So I have come down to rescue them from the hand of the Egyptians and to bring them up out of that land into a good and spacious land, a land flowing with milk and honey—the home of the Canaanites." (Exodus 3:7–8)

Laura Donaldson invites biblical interpreters to "read like a Canaanite," by recognizing the presence of others in the text who are not the primary focus of biblical authors.[23] From a postcolonial point of view, Israel can be viewed

---

20. Moore, *Empire and Apocalypse*, 31. See also Sugirtharajah, *The Bible and the Third World*, 259–61.

21. McKinlay, *Reframing Her*, viii.

22. Ibid.

23. Donaldson, *Postcolonialism and Bible Reading*, 11.

as both victim and perpetrator of colonialism/imperialism. Although the Exodus story is a paradigmatic exploration of freedom and liberation, it does not promote freedom and liberation for all. God sends the Israelites into the home of the Canaanites. The promised land is already occupied, albeit by a much maligned race. God's directive to the Israelites is at best to avoid other races, at worst, a directive to kill and destroy not only the Canaanite people but also their culture. A postcolonial exploration of this narrative considers the story from the point of view of the colonized, in this case, the Canaanites. The story takes on a different meaning if read from the position of Canaan's inhabitants, or indeed, if read from the perspective of any modern peoples whose land has been expropriated, such as the indigenous people of North America. When we listen to the voices not included in the text, the liberative meaning of the Exodus narrative is problematized.

The Great Justification for Conquest: Matthew 28:19–20a

> Go therefore and make disciples of all nations, baptizing them in the name of the Father and of the Son and of the Holy Spirit, and teaching them to obey everything I have commanded you. (Matthew 28:19–20a)

Postcolonial critics have investigated how Matthew 28:19–20a has been interpreted as a justification for entering and altering the land and cultures of others. It has contributed to the creation of Christian empires.[24] Sugirtharajah reinvestigates Matthew's commission in light of its use as a "biblical warrant to missionize the natives" in both the colonial and post-independence periods in India.[25] He indicates that this text was largely dormant during the Reformation period, but was invoked with increasing frequency during the eighteenth and nineteenth centuries, corresponding to the rise of Western imperialism.[26]

Musa Dube, a Botswanian scholar, challenges traditional Protestant interpretations of this passage, which she views as generally imperialist in nature. Matthew's commission, Dube claims, has been interpreted and enacted as a justification for uninvited border crossing. She suggests that

24. Peters, "Decolonizing our Minds," 99.
25. Sugirtharajah, *The Postcolonial Bible*, 95.
26. Ibid.

the command not only instructs followers of Jesus to travel into other lands without permission, but encourages one-way communication. According to Dube, the text "clearly implies that Christian disciples have a duty to teach all nations, without any suggestion that they must also in turn learn from all nations."[27]

The Gospel of Mark and Colonialism/Imperialism

As with the other gospels, Mark's gospel was written in the midst of the Roman Empire and describes the experience of persons living under colonial/imperial rule. As a case study for preachers developing their own response to colonizing discourse, the Gospel of Mark is a useful text to begin reflecting on Jesus' own situation in the midst of empire and the variety of possible responses possible to colonial/imperial leadership.

Richard Horsley argues that the Gospel of Mark can be viewed as a "submerged people's history," addressed to Greek-speaking, Gentile people who identified with the Jesus movement.[28] The very presence of poor and oppressed folk in the text may offer insight into the position of the Markan community. Economic and social issues displayed in the Gospel of Mark likely reflect the situation of Mark's community as a marginalized community oppressed by Roman imperial rule.

Roman military occupation was clearly a concern for Mark, as can be seen by the large number of colonial, imperial, and military references. Various characters attest to a colonial/imperial presence and the phenomenon of colonial/imperial collaboration: Levi and other tax collectors (2:13–17); King Herod (6:14, 8:15); officers at Herod's feast (6:21); the emperor (12:13–17); Pilate (15:1–15, 16:43–45); imperial soldiers (15:16–32); and the centurion at the foot of the cross (15:39). Mark's Jesus was tried in a colonial/imperial court and died on a colonial/imperial cross. Crucifixion was a cruel punishment practiced by the Roman authorities in response to insurgence, treason, or other political crimes.

What was the nature of colonial/imperial oppression in Jesus' Galilee? John Dominic Crossan paints a grim picture of exploited Galilean peasants: "They had no cash, they had little land, they paid their taxes and eked out a living, their bodies bore the scars of hard work, and they were despised."[29]

27. Dube, "Go Therefore and Make Disciples of all Nations," 224–25.

28. Horsley, *Hearing the Whole Story*, 30.

29. Crossan and Reed, *Excavating Jesus*, 21.

Land ownership was an area of profound tension between Galilee and Rome. Taxation and land appropriation resulted in a gradual enslaving of the peasants. Industry was under the authority of Rome, including the fishing industry, the produce of which benefited the ruling classes and elite imperial leaders.

In the time of Jesus, Roman rule was mediated by Herodian kingship and the temple priesthood, a state of affairs that further complicated the colonial/imperial situation. The beneficiaries of Roman domination were not only the Roman leaders and elites but also the local rulers and client kings, some of whom cooperated with Roman authority. For example, the temple leadership may have been indebted to the Roman colonizers for the tax revenues that were used to expand the temple, among other financial and security benefits.

Although the experience of Roman occupation in terms of economics and culture may have been different in upper and lower Galilee, both places shared a history of occupation and were simultaneously oppressed by Roman imperial ideology and the cooperation of local authorities with Roman authorities. This shared oppression created a particular space in which the original audience would have heard the words of Mark's Jesus. For example, Stephen Moore discusses Mark's use of *basileia*, or kingdom: "In any Roman province, the primary referent of *basileia* would have been the *imperium Romanum*."[30]

A growing number of scholars have examined the Gospel of Mark from a postcolonial perspective. The gospel is particularly fascinating in terms of the author's response to empire. A text produced in a colonial/imperial milieu is bound to express a response to colonial/imperial rule. Yet Mark's gospel expresses several responses. Some scholars view Mark's gospel as resistance literature, clear anticolonial rhetoric, in which Mark speaks from a peripheral position and aims to organize his audience to act against Roman oppression. The Markan narrative allows space for colonized peoples of varying social position to voice or act out concerns related to Roman occupation. Rome was only one of many imperial powers in the region's history, and its cultural identity had been repeatedly threatened. This history of colonization and domination by foreign powers may have created an ambiance of anticolonialism within the people of Galilee. Resistance to imperial projects is found deep in the Jewish

---

30. Moore, *Empire and Apocalypse*, 38.

tradition itself, especially within the stories and traditions surrounding the escape from Egypt.

Other scholars, however, maintain that the Markan text is not unequivocally anticolonial. Some suggest the author may have intended to resist colonial/imperial dominance, but ultimately reinscribes colonial/imperial power. Benny Liew argues that Mark copies, or mimics, the language and power of Roman Imperial ideology. Mark's portrayal of Jesus' status as God's only Son and heir results in "yet another hierarchical community structure," which mimics the authority of the Emperor.[31] Jesus has absolute authority in Mark, including power to define and direct the disciples. By attributing such absolute authority to Jesus, is Mark "deftly switching Jesus for Caesar?" Or, is Mark co-opting Roman terminology and ideology as a means of resistance? This is a process referred to as *catachresis*, "by which the colonized strategically appropriate and redeploy such specific elements of colonial or imperial culture or ideology."[32] Mark may be deliberately misusing Roman terminology for an alternative and subversive purpose. For example, by contrasting Roman authority with the authority of Jesus as the Son of God, the Gospel sets up a choice for readers. Which authority is legitimate? Will readers obey the Emperor, or Jesus Christ?

A third perspective claims that Mark is somewhat ambivalent in its response to colonialism/imperialism. There are portions of the Markan text that are explicitly pro- or anti-colonial, yet the gospel as a whole denotes a certain ambivalence toward Rome, a simultaneous repulsion and attraction. This is consistent with the intricate and often ambiguous nature of colonial/imperial relationships and power structures within the gospel, as well as the multiple responses available to colonized subjects. Mark's story of a colonized Jesus can be read as a discourse of a marginal and oppressed community that is simply trying to cope with the presence of an overwhelming authority. Mark's community is trying to find a space for itself between Roman colonial/imperial power and the segment of the Jewish population that seeks to ensure its own survival by collaborating with Rome. Mark takes a culturally in-between posture, and his narrative reflects a variety of responses to colonial/imperial subjugation. The gospel characters variously accommodate and resist Rome and its local collaborators, imitate their oppressors "with a difference," envision an alternative community, remain silent, or wait for God to act.

31. Liew, "The Gospel of Mark," 114.

32. Moore, *Empire and Apocalypse*, 37.

Jesus and the Syrophoenician Woman

> From there he set out and went away to the region of Tyre. He
> entered a house and did not want anyone to know he was there.
> Yet he could not escape notice, but a woman whose little daughter
> had an unclean spirit immediately heard about him, and she came
> and bowed down at his feet. Now the woman was a Gentile, of Sy-
> rophoenician origin. She begged him to cast the demon out of her
> daughter. He said to her, "Let the children be fed first, for it is not
> fair to take the children's food and throw it to the dogs." But she
> answered him, "Sir, even the dogs under the table eat the children's
> crumbs." Then he said to her, "For saying that, you may go—the
> demon has left your daughter." So she went home, found the child
> lying on the bed, and the demon gone. (Mark 7:24–30 NRSV)

The Syrophoenician Woman's story is a complex and disturbing narrative that resists easy categorization. It is a difficult text to read and preach,
yet it occurs in the lectionary cycle. Traditional interpretations of this text
are inadequate and rarely consider the broader political and economic context in which this story occurs. A postcolonial interpretive lens provides
fascinating insight into the actions of both Jesus and the woman, and it
highlights themes such as agency, land, resources, and border crossing.
The postcolonial reading developed here is neither systematic nor correct,
but interrogates the text and asks a different set of questions. The meeting
between Jesus and the Syrophoenician Woman produces a hybrid Third
Space in which healing occurs. In order to enter this space, both Jesus and
the woman cross boundaries and negotiate cultural difference, particularly
gender, race, and socioeconomic status. Thus, it is an encounter between
colonial subjects that provides a vivid scriptural account of the productive
possibility of the postcolonial Third Space.

Among the most challenging aspects of this passage is Jesus' initial refusal to heal the woman's daughter (7:27) as well as his seemingly irrelevant
reference to bread. The geopolitical and economic context provide insight.
Mark locates his story in Tyre, a region recorded as a threat to Israel in
several places in the Old Testament (Isa 23; Jer 47:4; Ezek 27, 28; Joel 3:4–8;
Zech 9:2). A non-Jewish city, Tyre was an ethnically mixed border town in
which Phoenician, Jewish, and Hellenistic culture coexisted.[33] There was
bitterness between Jews and Gentiles on the border between Tyre and Galilee. Tyre was on an island, thus, despite its wealth, its territory was limited,

---

33. Thiessen, *The Gospels in Context*, 68.

and it relied on imports of food and other resources from Galilee, resulting in a situation in which Jewish farmers were forced to sell their produce to the wealthy inhabitants of the cities, leaving little to feed their own families.

If the Syrophoenician Woman is rich, then she may be eating at the cost of the rural Jewish peasants who go hungry despite their heavy labor. This perspective changes the impact of Jesus' words to the woman, which might be read as: "first let the poor people in the Jewish rural areas be satisfied. For it is not good to take poor people's food and throw it to the rich Gentiles in the cities."[34]

Who are the masters who sit at the table with their deserving children, and who are the dogs underneath? Are the woman and her daughter the dogs because they are racially inferior to Jesus as one who belongs to the house of Israel?[35] Or are the Israelites peasants dogs, insofar as they were treated as such by the Roman authorities and Jewish leaders who collaborated with Rome and the urban elite of cities like Tyre, perhaps even the Syrophoenician Woman? In that case, the dogs represent Jesus' community, forced to seek sustenance underneath the master's table. In that case, "Jesus' household metaphor in which the bread goes first to the children of Israel would be understood by early listeners as a reversal of the reigning order."[36]

In the Markan narrative conflict between Jesus and leaders of Israel centers on physical and social boundaries, specifically those related to purity. For the Jewish leaders, boundaries must be carefully guarded in order to protect God's people from the uncleanness that might mar their holiness. Jesus redraws the boundaries between clean and unclean in particular as he approaches this woman who is Jesus' other, "not only geographically, but sexually, racially and religiously, on the outside."[37] Jesus, on the other hand, is "a traveller, whose divinity, class, race, and gender endow him with privilege and authority."[38] He is free to journey to another geographical location, but he is also a figure who has been rejected by those in authority, broken purity laws, eaten with outsiders, and occupies a low socioeconomic position. Like the woman, Jesus is an outsider, and at least from the perspective of his more orthodox opponents, he too is polluted.

---

34. Ibid., 75.

35. Dube, *Postcolonial Feminist Interpretation*, 147.

36. Hicks, "Moral Agency at the Borders," 83.

37. Perkinson, "A Canaanitic Word," 69.

38. Dube, *Postcolonial Feminist Interpretation*, 146.

Mark's Jesus and the Syrophoenician Woman each make a choice to enter into an exchange despite social and cultural proprieties. The woman does things she should not do, even breaking the boundary of gender. She is the only woman in Mark's Gospel to engage in conversation with Jesus. It is culturally inappropriate for her to approach him and ask for a favor, yet Jesus does not dispute the freedom of this woman to cross cultural boundaries. Jesus may himself have recognized the changeable boundaries of otherness in Israel's tradition: "On the question of the Other, the foreigner, the (biblical) narratives are decidedly inconsistent. . . . Who is an outsider is perpetually negotiated."[39]

Jesus and the woman ignore multiple social and political borderlines, and act subversively. Their breaking of boundaries results in a new space where healing occurs. In the end, the unclean daughter is healed. Such a healing, occurring across social boundaries, can be interpreted as an act of resistance against the social and political powers that seek to keep persons separate.

The space between Jesus and the woman is not neutral space, it is "already filled with a particular discourse of domination,"[40] and the Roman Empire is an unspoken presence in this space. The roles of Jesus and the woman are socially defined and seem to make an antagonistic encounter inevitable. Colonialism/imperialism often pit colonized persons against one another. Aside from gender and religion, "economic dependence, political expansionism and cultural distance provided a fertile soil for aggressive prejudices on both sides."[41] Yet this encounter breaks the limits of discourse that have been predetermined by social, religious, and political boundaries, and results in transformation.

Hybridity can be perceived as an act of protest against forces that seek to maintain cultural and religious purity. Hybridities break all the rules of purity. When Jesus crossed boundaries of space and purity, bringing together clean and unclean, sinner and righteous, the religious authorities protested. In the Gospel of Mark, immediately before Jesus travels to Tyre and encounters the Syrophoenician Woman, he is engaged in a controversy with some scribes and Pharisees regarding eating with defiled hands (7:1–23). In that discussion, Jesus redefines defilement and impurity, and declares all foods clean. He argues that the words and actions issuing from an

---

39. Schwartz, *The Curse of Cain*, 197.
40. Perkinson, "A Canaanitic World," 74.
41. Thiessen, *The Gospels in Context*, 76.

individual will make him or her unclean, not what is put into the body. It is perhaps no surprise Jesus is willing and able to encounter a hybrid woman, in a hybrid territory, and participate in a healing that cleanses the unclean. Postcolonial hybridity denies the possibility of unadulterated purity. Thus, the woman and Jesus were not crossing carved-in-stone boundaries, but recognizing fluidity and impurity as normative.

As Jesus and the woman choose to cross boundaries, they enter into a Third Space, a fluid and dynamic space in which healing and transformation occur. Mark 7:24–30 has been interpreted as a sign of God's welcome to the outsider—the acceptance of the Gentile into Israel's history of salvation. This interpretation is understandable given that Jesus goes out of his way to be hospitable to a Gentile woman. Yet Kwok Pui-lan argues against a too-hasty baptism of the woman as a Gentile Christian "without acknowledging the different culture and tradition she represents."[42] We are quick to place the woman into familiar categories, but to do so reflects a reductionist and simplified understanding of cultural difference. It is not clear from the text that she chooses to change her religious affiliation or daily lived experience in response to her daughter's healing. The healing occurs despite her difference, despite the fact she crosses boundaries and represents impurity. The choice, whether to follow Jesus or not, and on whose terms, is left in her hands. Envisioning this encounter as a Third Space encounter allows for the woman and Jesus to meet, to change each other, but not be incorporated into the same category or made same. They are allowed to maintain cultural difference. Ideological conflicts between these two individuals and the communities they represent have not disappeared, nor are they swept under the rug. The tension in the air does not evaporate. Jesus does not object to the Syrophoenician Woman's right to signify, her right to represent herself on her own terms. This text demonstrates what may happen when space is made for conversation with one who is truly other.

As an illustrative category, Third Space provides food for thought but must be approached with caution. Is the Third Space safe from colonization? Like a colonizer, Jesus has power over someone who is in the distance (the sick daughter), and he exerts control over the body of another without her consent or her permission. To be sure, the healing is a welcome and positive act, but it remains, in some ways, an act of control.

A postcolonial imagination offers space for such difficult questions, but the presence of difficult questions does not nullify the possibility of a

---

42. Kwok, *Discovering the Bible*, 82.

space in which reconciliation and healing can occur. My interpretation of this passage recognizes the speech of the other has power. The Syrophoenician Woman's speech, "her saying," enacts change and healing. Jesus' last words to the woman are ambiguous. "For saying that, you may go—the demon has left your daughter" (7:29). It is not clear whose word actually caused the healing,[43] only that the words were issued in the complex space between Jesus and the woman. This is grace-filled ambiguity. While I affirm that healing comes from God, this passage also suggests God works in and through unexpected persons and encounters.

Including Postcolonial Reading Strategies in Exegetical Toolbox

"Trying to understand Jesus' speech and action without knowing how Roman imperialism determined the conditions of life in Galilee and Jerusalem would be like trying to understand Martin Luther King without knowing how slavery, reconstruction, and segregation determined the lives of African-Americans in the United States."[44] Colonialism/imperialism is part and parcel of the biblical text and the context in which we interpret that text. Most preachers have a particular process for approaching texts for preaching. To include postcolonial reading strategies in one's exegetical toolbox is not to discard the usual process, but to bring different questions to the text and to the preacher's own context. By employing a modified form of postcolonial biblical criticism in sermon preparation, preachers can identify colonizing discourse within the text and adequately consider the colonial/imperial context of the biblical text. The intent is not to seek a correct or universal reading, but to develop a deeper understanding.

Postcolonial biblical criticism entails "not only a systematic accounting of Christianity's participation in imperialism, but also that individual congregations actively become involved in a more direct manner."[45] By employing postcolonial scriptural interpretation in sermons, preachers and listeners are challenged with a new way of interpreting the text and the contemporary situation, and they are enabled to recognize and respond to colonizing discourse today.

43. Perkinson, "A Canaanitic Word," 77.
44. Horsley, *Jesus and Empire*, 13.
45. Donaldson, *Postcolonialism and Bible Reading*, 2.

Part III: A Toolbox for Decolonizing Preaching

The following questions are designed to challenge both the text and the preacher from a postcolonial perspective and provide a relatively simple aid for developing sermons that reflect a postcolonial imagination and a Social Trinitarian theology. There is no checklist to be followed, but these guidelines are intended to uncover the colonial/imperial situation of the text and the author's response to that situation, and bring to bear several categories often underused in traditional exegetical processes. There are questions to ask of the text and questions designed to aid the movement from text to sermon (in italics).

Exegetical Questions to Engage a Postcolonial Imagination

1. What is the colonial/imperial context of the text's author, audience, and characters? Is there any direct reference to the empire in this text? *Identify the colonial/imperial context of preacher and listeners.*

2. What is the history of interpretation of this text? Has this text been used to justify colonial/ imperial domination? *Does this sermon encourage any kind of colonial or imperial domination? Does this sermon encourage action that impinges on the land or culture of others?*

3. Colonizing discourse: does it appear in the text? *Do I perceive in the text, or in my reaction to the text, engagement in colonizing discourse that seeks to dominate, separate, homogenize, or close off future possibility or essentialize identity? What does this text say to colonizing discourse as it occurs in the world my listeners and I inhabit?*

4. How does the text represent the identities of various biblical characters? *How will I represent these identities and differences in my sermon?*

5. What happens in the encounters between and among biblical characters, the in-between spaces? *How will my sermon function as a space in which listeners can encounter others on their own terms? Might this space be threatening or dangerous to my listeners? Can this space be made safe? Which others does this text challenge us to respond to?*

6. What categories are relevant to interpreting this text (geography, land, economics, power, agency, borders or boundaries, difference, culture)?

7. Is this a text/perspective I want to applaud and collude with or resist?[46] *In my sermon, will I take a stand against the colonial oppression in the text and the imperial realities in our world?*

46. McKinlay, *Reframing Her*, xiii.

Conclusion

When we read our sacred Scriptures with postcolonial lenses, "these biblical writings spur those of us who read them and study them to further conversations . . . reminding us that 'gender', 'identity', and 'difference' are always, and must always be, under negotiation.'"[47]

For the preacher, a postcolonial hermeneutic may be an uncomfortable acquisition. Not only will postcolonial interpretations challenge us to adjust our behavior and identity, we will need to find new language and images to replace what is familiar and comfortable. "It is shocking and disorienting to be confronted with angles of vision that contest dominant assumptions, making it impossible to interpret a story in familiar ways."[48] The interpretive style just proposed will change the way we engage with Scripture and will therefore change the way we preach. Even familiar texts will take on an unfamiliar hue. For example, Mark 12:41–44 tells the story of a widow's offering. This passage is often used as an exhortation to faithfulness and generosity—especially suited to stewardship Sunday! Yet a postcolonial reading of this passage offers an entirely different perspective. Such a reading might engage the widow's story from the widow's point of view. The story may not be a straightforward affirmation of the woman's offering, but an "exposure of abuse by the temple treasury authorities."[49] The widow gives all she has, which is almost nothing, in order to support a corrupt temple system. Even worse, it is the responsibility of the temple authorities and others to care for the needy widow. Interpreted in this way, the story serves as a recognition of the failure of the whole system to obey the law. Jesus is not simply acknowledging her generosity, but calling into question the righteousness of the authorities who should know better.

Ultimately, a postcolonial hermeneutic for preaching will mean we cease to protect the boundaries of our own space and invite others to enter. In the same way, we hope for the privilege and opportunity to enter the space of others, so that between self and other, between God's word in the text and God's word in the sermon, we may find grace.

47. Ibid., 167.
48. Donaldson, *Postcolonialism and Bible Reading*, 12.
49. Sugirtharajah, *Postcolonial Criticism and Biblical Interpretation*, 121.

7

Preaching in Trinitarian Embrace

ORLD WAR I DIVIDED the Western world. It was a conflict
played out in trenches and mud, barbed wire and close combat. Young men, grown weary of the endless waiting and
tension, began to wonder whether the opposing side was really as evil as
portrayed by the propaganda of their own governments. On Christmas
Eve 1914, along the Western Front, perhaps nostalgic for home during the
holiday season, perhaps out of boredom or a sense of Christmas spirit that
invaded even the muddy trenches, soldiers began to behave in unexpected
ways. German and Allied soldiers began to sing Christmas carols, clearly
audible across enemy lines. At dawn on Christmas Day, some German soldiers entered no-man's land, calling out Christmas greetings. The Allied
troops responded in their own languages. Emboldened by these signs of
humanity and mutual identification, the men from both sides of the conflict gathered in the space between the trenches. They played cards, traded
goods, joined in a spontaneous soccer game. While only a brief respite in
a brutal war, these soldiers found a common space in which to recognize
their shared humanity and in some small way resist the engines of empire
that had lured them to the trenches in the first place.

This image of a space in-between is a provocative and powerful image
for postcolonial reflection. What is possible in the space between preacher
and listener? In the space between North and South? In the space between
colonizer and colonized? Face-to-face encounters, even figurative encounters may sometimes interrupt prevailing discourses. Encounters among
those who perceived themselves to dwell at the center of God's life in Trinity
hold even more potential. When individuals or groups come into proximity

126

with one another in the embrace of the Holy Trinity, life and healing are made possible, even in the midst of empire and the continued expression of colonizing discourse.

The postcolonial approach to preaching I have constructed is built on a particular image of God. The Trinity is a theological foundation for the kind of preaching that addresses the oppression of empire and seeks to repair and reimagine human relationships that have been torn apart by colonialism/imperialism. The Trinity, even as it is articulated in Social Trinitarian theology, is a challenging concept to apply to daily life. It is a deep and dense theological proposal. However, the social doctrine of the Trinity also provides a concrete and visual representation of God's life together and the participation of humanity in that divine life. Creator, Son, and Holy Spirit exist in a loving relationship free from domination, mutually considerate, tolerant of difference, and open to the whole of creation. A corresponding visual image places Creator, Son, and Holy Spirit into a circle, each moving around and into the others in a perichoretic dance. At the center of this divine circle is a space—a living space, a space made within God's own self for the created order. All of creation, including humanity, dwells within the space of God's embrace. In this space, there is possibility for human relationships characterized by a similar freedom, mutuality, diversity, and openness.

This space within the Trinity corresponds to another space—the Third Space conjectured by postcolonial theory. The Third Space is a location in which community and identity are negotiated and where postcolonial subjects can enter into discourse not bound to the typical boundaries of colonizing discourse. It is a space of creativity in which new truths can be uttered and existing perceptions of truth can be disputed, rejected, altered, or explained. Hybridity, rather than a condition to be managed carefully as viewed by the colonial/imperial system, is recognized as normative. Homi K. Bhabha has argued that this space has opened up as the discourses of modernity have failed, creating the possibility of new systems, languages, and relationships. While in many ways a symbolic space, it is a space brought to life in culturally mixed societies—in our nations, cities, and churches. The possibility of a Third Space opens up when difference encounters difference. For a number of reasons, this space might evaporate before it is occupied—we may choose not to enter, or prefer to maintain strict boundaries between self and other. The possibility, however, of a postcolonial space in which colonizing discourses can be challenged and changed is a tantalizing one.

The Perichoretic Space

The space of the Trinity, the space of postcolonial theory—these can be fruitfully brought together to describe a dynamic space in which postcolonial preaching occurs. Trinitarian love, in contradiction to the inequality, separation, segregation, homogeneity, and essentialism of colonizing discourse, creates the possibility of a Third Space in which hybridity, cultural impurity, boundary crossing, and mixedness are permitted. Not only is hybridity permitted, by the grace of the Triune God hybridity can lead to healing and transformation. Thus, the boundaries and spaces and gaps between us are opened up as a Third Space in which God transforms the boundaries among groups and individuals. Remember the example of Jesus and the Syrophoenician Woman from chapter 6. These two highly disparate characters engage one another in conversation despite their profound differences and the presence of political, cultural, and religious boundaries. A new, hybrid space opens between them that challenges any notion of cultural purity, and in which a healing word is spoken and the woman's daughter is made well. Although it is unclear in the text from whom the healing word issues, I interpret the healing to indicate divine presence and power at the point of contact between Jesus and the woman. This Third Space encounter can be conceptualized as a Venn diagram. The separate circles come together to create an overlap. While there is still tension and potential antagonism, there is a hybrid and ambiguous space in which communication becomes possible, and the relationship may be moved in a more positive direction through conversation and the presence of the Triune God.

If we imagine Third Space encounters to be located within a Trinitarian space, these encounters are not limited to the human persons or groups involved. Rather, they are indwelled by the Triune God, and thus opened to a Trinitarian discourse that deconstructs all other discourse. All binaries and us-versus-them are interrupted and decentered by the divine presence. At odds with the territorialism of colonialism and cultural imperialism, Third Spaces do not belong to one or the other, to the Tricontinent or to the West, to the colonizer or colonized or observers. These spaces belong to God-in-Trinity. In fact, the space itself is located within the Trinity. Center, middle, and periphery are dislocated because all are loved equally by the Triune God and are equally dependent on Trinitarian grace.

Christian self-understanding and understanding of others is related to the perception of the nature of divine community and the perichoretic, kenotic love of the Triune God both in divine circulation and the manner in which it reaches toward humanity. In these Third Spaces, our identities and our understanding of others' identities are formed and reformed through complex interactions among self, others, and the Triune God. Identity is not fixed, but is open to change and transformation, engaged in a continuing process of becoming. The very presence of others in this space will change how we define ourselves. For example, input from those who have been colonized challenges the dominant Western construction of self. The Syrophoenician Woman speaks and challenges Jesus' spoken construction of Israel. We come to see ourselves through the eyes of others, which may lead to a new and profoundly different understanding of who we are, as well as our perception of both history and the future. The binaries and antagonism inherent to colonizing discourse are not reflective of the reality of lived experience, which is varied and ambiguous. Both binaries and antagonism are foreign to Trinitarian discourse. Instead of being defined in opposition to others or in terms of sameness or homogeneous identity, those who occupy the Perichoretic Space are defined by *imago trinitatis*. Instead of confronting others as oppressed or oppressor, the possibility arises for us to become engaged in a common struggle against the structures of oppression and domination that attempt to hold all of us captive. Rather than the violent resistance and counter-resistance of colonialism/imperialism, the suffering love of Trinity draws us toward one another and invites us to imitate the love that suffers with and for others.

In Third Space encounters, we are invited to give of ourselves to others (self-giving) and make space for them within ourselves (other-receiving). As the Triune God changes the nature of colonizing discourse and heals the wounds of fear and anger that may exist between us, others may reciprocate by giving of self and receiving us into themselves. The power of God, working in these spaces, creates the possibility of friendship. Moltmann views friendship as a relationship of self-giving characterized by freedom, respect, affection, and loyalty. Friendship and love emerge from the human experience of being loved by the Trinity. We learn how to love and befriend neighbor and stranger because we have known the infinite generosity of Trinitarian embrace.[1]

Such friendship may be practiced across cultures, by groups or communities as well as individuals. Through a Trinitarian understanding of identity, communities divided by geography or other factors can recognize

---

1. McDougall, *Pilgrimage of Love*, 144.

one another. A common identity rooted in Creator, Son, and Spirit allows friendship to develop despite barriers and boundaries.[2] While human relationships rarely work this way, in the space of the Social Trinity it is possible to imagine these friendships as an alternative to antagonistic or violent encounters. Friendships are relationships that stand in stark contrast to the relationships formed by colonizing discourse.

According to Miroslav Volf, the Christian self is always inhabited or indwelled by others, and is in this sense qualified by others.[3] We have already been opened to one another by virtue of our membership in Christ's body. Thus, we cannot be perceived to be entirely independent, but mutually dependent. Making space for others is a generous and hospitable act in which we allow others to enter our lives as we enter theirs. This is not the one-way forced entry of colonialism/imperialism, but a mutual relationship made possible by God's demonstration of perichoretic love.

Preaching in the Perichoretic Space names colonialism/imperialism in both past and present, exposes colonizing discourse in the church and beyond, and deconstructs and reorients colonizing discourse. In the Perichoretic Space, preachers are free to critique empires and colonizing discourses, all of which are revealed to be illusory in the face of the Triune God.

Preaching in the Perichoretic Space

The previous chapters have offered concrete hermeneutical, exegetical, and research strategies for postcolonial preaching. A truly postcolonial approach to preaching not only employs strategies but is built upon a solid theological foundation that undergirds all other strategies and creates the ethos in which we approach and construct sermons. From the perspective of Social Trinitarian theology, our preaching and worship belong to the life of the Trinity. Thus, worship spaces are filled not only with discourses of power such as colonizing discourse but also with love and grace and the potential for transformative reconciliation. We gather as a community formed and created to be in the image of the Trinity, *imago trinitatis*. Even as we acknowledge our profound failings and inability to reflect God's image perfectly, we have been created to reach toward God and toward one another. We have been designed to participate in the life of self-giving love that characterizes the dynamic space of divine fellowship that extends and

2. Moltmann, *The Church in the Power of the Spirit*, 343.

3. Volf, *After Our Likeness*, 3.

surrounds human community. In these spaces, we are prepared by Word and sacrament to participate in the mission of God. We are sent out toward our Christian brothers and sisters, but also to engage in a discourse with a multiplicity of others within the communities in which we live and move, as well as the broader global community.

Preachers exist in this Perichoretic Space and address particular communities of listeners also dwelling in the Perichoretic Space. The community addressed by preaching is a temporal and fallible community constructed not only by Trinitarian discourse but also by the particular historical discourses in which it has developed and continues to dwell. This community is related to others within the global church and beyond, insofar as we understand God to be the sovereign creator, Jesus as the one sent to reconcile all people to God and one another, and the Holy Spirit as the inspiration for communal life. Thus, we are linked to others across time and space. The Perichoretic Space, then, is profoundly other-oriented rather than selfish, individualistic, or self-protective.

Preaching in this space involves an act of theological imagination. Preachers are invited to develop an awareness of their own location in the Perichoretic Space, their Trinitarian identity, and the potentially transforming power of the Social Trinity's discourse. As preachers learn to discern and respond to the discourse of the Social Trinity, they are gifted with an enlarged and profoundly other-oriented vision of the ministry of the church. Having experienced for themselves the transforming power of Trinitarian discourse, preachers invite listeners into deeper awareness of their collective location in the Perichoretic Space. Preachers and listeners will confront various questions in the sermon and within the broader conversation of the congregation: what does it mean for a particular community of faith to reflect, or mirror, God's life-in-Trinity? What is an appropriate response to those sitting next to us and those occupying distant space who may or may not share our own faith and cultural commitments? In what way have our utterances been at odds with Trinitarian discourse in the past?

Much postcolonial scholarship has targeted identity as a key theme and challenge of postcolonial reality. Identity, in the wake of colonialism/imperialism, is a fluid concept. While colonizers have traditionally attempted to suppress indigenous identity and implant the identity of the colonizer, colonized persons have responded by resisting the identities imposed upon them, seeking to regain or reimagine their own identities. For all of us who live in the ethos of empire, identity remains a key issue. In a hybrid world, it becomes more and more difficult to comprehend or agree on national identities. In the church, we are caught in an identity crisis. Are we citizens of empire, or citizens of the kingdom of God? Can both exist simultaneously? Can we serve both Caesar and the living God? The daily reality for preachers and listeners is that we struggle to incorporate both identities. It is very difficult, if not impossible, to disengage entirely from the demands of empire—we are utterly reliant on military, financial, and consumer cultures. There are, however, opportunities to make choices for or against full participation in empire. Our response to others is one aspect of our identity and behavior that is fully within our prerogative. In addition, our position within the Perichoretic Space allows for a vantage point from which to critique the demands and expectations of empire. We need not accept or participate uncritically in the systems of empire, including those who have produced and sustained colonizing discourse. Such discourse simply does not belong in the Perichoretic Space. An awareness of the call to live in *imago trinitatis*, and the church's situation within the Perichoretic Space will be followed by a restructuring of communal identity. Who are we as a people of God if we are defined and shaped by God's own identity? This is an other-oriented identity, deeply concerned with the well-being of proximate and distant others. Sermons can problematize easy accommodation to the demands of empire, and develop our skill to live in between—as citizens of one empire, created and shaped for life in another, the kingdom of God. Through a process of interrelation with the Persons of the Trinity, we discover who we are and what is expected of us.

Our identity as children of God dwelling in the Perichoretic Space is an identity that can be nurtured by the practice of preaching. Such preaching, however, need not fully separate or entirely differentiate listeners from those whose lives are shaped by other commitments. If we understand ourselves according to the characteristics of God-in-Trinity, then our goal is not to be separated from the world around us. Instead, preaching equips us to dwell in a Third Space where God works to make connections and brings about the possibility of healing and reconciliation. This matters for how we relate to others and how we understand the church's mission. Mission is an action of the Triune God in which humans participate. I understand mission in a broad sense, inclusive of the manner in which local Christian communities care for others—Christian and non-Christian, near and far. It is an act of self-giving love that flows out toward one's other. This view of mission arises out of the ecumenical consensus of the twentieth century, which established the importance of the *Missio Dei* for a theological understanding of mission. Letty Russell offers a useful synopsis of mission as *Missio Dei* rooted in the Trinity:

> God's sending action is the work of the economic Trinity in caring for God's world house, the *oikos*. Through this action Christians come to know God's presence, and speak of God within God's self (the immanent Trinity) as a dynamic relationship of love and sharing between God, Christ and the Holy Spirit. The mission is God's and the calling of the Church is to participate in that mission as a postscript on God's love affair with the world.[4]

Sermons, by increasing the church's capacity to speak meaningfully about power and difference, can participate in breaking down the barriers that prevent fruitful communication and self-giving within the church and beyond.

A Trinitarian theological vision opens a pathway by which preachers can publicly dispute colonizing discourse. It is helpful to revisit the primary categories with which I described the character of the Social Trinity. Sermons that aim to develop a Trinitarian identity will be careful to speak against any forms of domination that limit the freedom of others. In fact, they will hope for the freedom of others even if it means a restriction in the freedom of the self. Such sermons will encourage self-giving and communication. They will attempt to ease the panic that may arise among listeners regarding the "dissolution of essential identity categories."[5] In other words, listeners may struggle with the manner in which identity has changed over time—the identity of the church, national identity, their own identity. The resulting disorientation may cause some to desire a more clear delineation of boundaries between one person and another, one group and another. Yet preaching can help redraw the boundaries between persons and groups, replacing concrete walls with permeable borderlands that allow entry into the Third Space. Life in Trinity dispels a historically driven shame of mixedness. To affirm mixedness is an act of subversion—a refusal to let the demands of empire separate those who have been brought together in the same space. Realities such as immigration and the mixing of races and ethnicities are a consequence of colonialism/imperialism. Yet the very nature of God affirms such mixedness, difference, and hybridity. We, as citizens of the Perichoretic Space, can choose to value rather than eschew difference.

4. Russell, "God, Gold, Glory and Gender," 42.
5. González, "Who is Americana/o," 68.

A sermon given by Desmond Tutu illustrates how the preacher's theological vision works to deconstruct the apartheid system. He contrasts apartheid with the biblical priority of reconciliation:

> Do I still need to demonstrate that apartheid is evil after all that I have said about the centrality for the Bible of unity and reconciliation? . . . The Bible declares right at the beginning that human beings are created in the image and likeness of God. I showed why this fact endows each person with a unique and infinite value, a person whose very hairs are numbered. And what makes any human being valuable therefore is not any biological characteristic. No, it is the fact that he or she is created in the image and likeness of God. Apartheid exalts a biological quality, which is a total irrelevancy, to the status of what determines the value, worth, of a human being. . . . Secondly, the chief work that Jesus came to perform on earth can be summed up by the word "Reconciliation." He came to restore human community and brotherhood which sin destroyed. He came to say that God has intended us for fellowship, for *koinonia*, for togetherness, without destroying our distinctiveness, our cultural otherness. Apartheid quite deliberately denies and repudiates this central act of Jesus and says we are made for separateness, for disunity, for enmity, for alienation, which we have shown to be the fruits of sin.[6]

Tutu explicitly names apartheid as contrary to God's purpose for humanity. Preachers point to the nature of God-in-Trinity in order to demonstrate how colonialism/imperialism are contrary to a Christian, Trinitarian theological vision. A particular sermon might name the ongoing effects of cultural imperialism upon First Nations peoples or the continuing presence of racism in the church and society. The willingness of congregations to tolerate or even participate in these realities can be contrasted with God's invitation to participate in Trinitarian life. When our ears are filled with the discourse of a loving Trinity, we begin to long for a discourse of love rather than discourses of power. Moltmann writes, "Those who hope in Christ can no longer put up with reality as it is, but begin to suffer under it, to contradict it."[7] The fellowship of the divine community results in "a questioning of all reality that does not reflect the ideal of *perichoresis* as Trinitarian life."[8]

6. Tutu, "The Divine Intention," 166–67.

7. Moltmann, *Theology of Hope*, 21.

8. Bonzo, *Indwelling and the Forsaken Other*, 91.

Colonial/imperial reality does not reflect the perichoretic ideal—it is therefore to be called into question by the ecclesial community in communion with the Triune God. This invites a willingness on the part of Christians to repent for conscious or unconscious colonial/imperial collaboration. At times we will stand in judgment of the past—not because we know better, but because we exist at the heart of the Triune God, where we have witnessed a better way and been empowered to live in the *imago trinitatis*. In the context of Trinity, we are connected not only to one another in the contemporary global church, but also to others, across time and space, who sit at table in the kingdom of God. The Perichoretic Space, as the location of preaching, transcends the here and now, transcends time and space. It is in this perichoretic, eschatological space that "the Church dares to celebrate that which it does not possess, to 'represent' that which it does not own, and to proclaim a word that is not of this world."[9]

Reconciliation and Forgiveness

Reconciliation and recreation are embodied in sermons that proclaim that the body of Christ, the church, is not limited to what it has been. God is continually re-creating. In the Perichoretic Space, preachers look for and point to signs of transformation, reconciliation, and forgiveness in the church and world. Colonialism/imperialism and other damaging systems are an irrefutable reality in human history. It is impossible to change what has already occurred. Of course, these systems are not entirely negative and have resulted in the current world order, some of which is to be enjoyed and celebrated. Many of us enjoy the fruits of hybridity and immigration. I love the variety and diversity within the Canadian context, even as I recognize it comes at a cost and requires skillful navigation at times. Colonizing discourse, however, especially as it is measured against the loving nature of the Trinity, is a tragic continuing consequence of empire.

Is there room for redemption? Can God repair and reconcile those who have been forcefully divided by colonizing discourse? Can the love of the Trinity build new relationships among those whose lives have collided in unexpected ways? While acknowledging the ways in which humans have ignored, oppressed, or destroyed others throughout human history, preaching in the Perichoretic Space affirms God has another purpose for humanity. The hope, the certainty that God will ultimately work all things

9. Westhelle, *The Church Event*, 120.

for good is a hope that can reshape the distorted communities of the present age. God-in-Trinity continually pursues and embraces us, an embrace that anticipates what is to come. The eschatological hope for a new order contains possibilities that exceed our present vision. This hope affirms, along with postcolonial theology, that "such a post is possible."[10]

Richard Lischer writes about the "reconciling imperative" of preaching.[11] God has entrusted to us the message of reconciliation (2 Cor. 5:19). Lischer states, "what God has done, on both a macro- and microcosmic scale, is reconciliation."[12] In Bonhoeffer's words, "we are separated from one another by an unbridgeable gulf of otherness and strangeness which resists all our attempts to overcome it by means of natural association or emotional or spiritual union. There is no way from one person to another."[13] Yet preachers proclaim the good news of our reconciliation to the Triune God through Jesus Christ. This is a reconciling action that continues within the human community. As Lischer notes, "The reconciling sermon begins with pastoral discernment of the way things are. And the way things are is that many of us are living in the presence of our enemies. We preach reconciliation amidst a jumble of unfinished business, among people who are beginning new lives willy-nilly without having completed the old."[14] Thus, we can only preach toward reconciliation,[15] in faith that reconciliation is part of the Triune God's *creatio continua*. God's people are engaged in a process that moves us beyond the past and into new relationships.

The Perichoretic Space is a space of forgiveness. In God's mercy we are freed from our past sins and freed for a new kind of identity defined by the self-giving, other-receiving love of the Trinity. In this space, preachers proclaim God's forgiveness, as well as issue the gospel invitation to forgive one another as we have been forgiven. As we encounter human others in the Perichoretic Space, forgiveness becomes a distinct possibility. To borrow an image from Lischer, I imagine as we come face to face with others, "in the combustion of word and touch, miniature 'new creations' are exploding around the sanctuary."[16] Not only within the sanctuary but all over the

---

10. Keller, *Postcolonial Theologies*, xi.

11. Lischer, *The End of Words*, 132.

12. Ibid.

13. Bonhoeffer, *The Cost of Discipleship*, 140.

14. Lischer, *The End of Words*, 144.

15. Ibid., 148.

16. Ibid., 151.

global church, wherever colonizing discourse lurks it is potentially pushed aside by these explosions of grace and forgiveness. This message of reconciliation and forgiveness is vital for postcolonial preaching. In Lischer's words, "celebrating God's reconciliation of enemies in the church and the world" is the ultimate gospel gesture, and must be part of sermons that seek reconciliation.[17]

In October 1967, Jürgen Moltmann preached a sermon on World Communion Sunday based on Galatians, which addressed Christian identity and divisions in the church.[18] Fear and anxiety cause humanity to divide into groups of equals, often to unite against a common foe. This sermon points to the possibility of new creation for the church. Moltmann speaks of the love of God in Jesus Christ, which is the source of true human freedom:

> It is a love which seeks the lost and creates new life where otherwise hate kills everything. Through Christ we learn of this new creative love because we experience it only in Him. If we are recreated to a new life because of this love, we are enabled to love our enemies. I think this is the creative reality of the Christian community. Here our boundaries are infiltrated and the walls of separation men themselves erect from mutual isolation are raised.[19]

He names the church as the "advance guard of the coming new world of God," and goes on:

> It is true that what we are able to realize in this life are fragments beginning with only very small steps, but it belongs to the vision of the Christian hope to see the fragments of the coming whole: in the ambiguous beginning, in the unequivocal perfection, and in the earthen vessel, the beauty of the coming kingdom of God. What we are able to realize as kindness and peace in our Christian community is always very human and puny . . . but at the same time, this reality is a sacrament of great hope for the future.[20]

Creation has not yet been fully reconciled. The questions surrounding apology and forgiveness are more fully developed than the answers. In the face of historical cultural and ecclesial wrongdoing, what can the Western Church possibly say to its victims? Is it possible to atone for the

17. Ibid., 153.

18. Moltmann, "Communion Mediation."

19. Ibid., 84.

20. Ibid.

acts of colonialism/imperialism and if so, what is required? To what extent are the consequences of these past acts the responsibility of those of us who were not alive and did not make the decisions? Who is guilty? In some ways, the best we can do in the Perichoretic Space is view the past with a sense of sorrow. The bulk of our guilt and shame belongs to our participation in colonizing discourse in the here and now. We cannot change the past. We can make reparations to some extent. But there is perhaps no greater tribute to the victims of colonial/imperial oppression than a commitment to change the future—to learn a new discourse that challenges the discourses of power and domination. To live fully into our Trinitarian nature by rejecting and opposing all systems that oppress and divide. Those of us living in this postcolonial world cannot bear all the guilt for what has been done and what has gone wrong. Yet in the profoundly other-oriented space in the midst of Trinity, we discover we are responsible for the well-being of one another.

The Perichoretic Space is a location of possibility and hope. God's continuing acts of re-creation open the possibility of humanity coming fully to itself. In this space, the Triune God gives us a hope and vision of fellowship that leads to a particular orientation to others—a desire for others to be free, for mutual exchange, for valuing difference, and for an openness to the voice of others, human and divine.

Postcolonial Discourse In Between

Encounters within the Perichoretic Space do not banish colonizing discourse once and forever, but deconstruct colonizing discourse and unmask it as idolatrous. The Trinity's act of *creatio continua* alters and reorients colonizing discourse toward a more profoundly Trinitarian discourse. In the in-between Third Space, even as it is located in the relative safety of Perichoretic Space, there is tension and risk. While a certain degree of acceptance is assumed within the Perichoretic Space, this does not mean we must approve of all aspects of another person or culture. Nor should we become the other. There are some things we will choose not to condone. Neither is it a space where identity blurs to the point of losing all meaning. In fact, Christians are more fully themselves, more fully defined in this space—not in opposition to others, but in relation to God. Confident in our position within divine embrace, this is a relatively safe space in which to encounter otherness. In the words of missiologist David Bosch, "Without my commitment to the gospel, dialogue becomes a mere chatter; without the authentic practice of the neighbor it becomes arrogant and worthless."[21] It is our commitment to live in the image of the Trinity that gives us the freedom to explore the possibility of relationship and reconciliation with others, a freedom severely limited within the discourse of empire.

Notions of hybridity and Third Space must also be employed with caution. The very idea of oppressors occupying the same space as the oppressed is fraught with echoes of occupied territories. Historically, these have been "sites of coercion and resistance, and not of civil negotiation between evenly placed contenders."[22] Although we may desire to enter Third Spaces with neighbors or global partners, we must not forget the power inequalities, lest we reinscribe the very intrusive act of colonization itself. Acknowledging the complexity of colonial/imperial relationships, those who occupy relatively marginal positions might be reluctant to enter the same in-between space with those whom they perceive as oppressors, just as those implicated in colonial/imperial oppression may be reluctant to face those who perceive themselves to be victims.

The Perichoretic Space will not feel like a safe space for those who have been oppressed and hurt. The response of others is never predictable, and there is always risk involved in human encounters. For very good reason, colonized persons, victims of colonizing discourse, will be reluctant to enter into any kind of relationship with those who have abused power or have been associated with abuses of power.

The anger, fear, and suspicion inspired by colonizing discourse do not simply evaporate, and there is a need for active participation by the Church in identifying and working to ease both relational and material effects of colonizing discourse. Brad Braxton comments, "reconciliation is often depicted as an embrace or hug that overcomes hostility. But hugging a person bleeding profusely without attending to the gaping wound is more of a kiss of death than a hug to end hostility."[23] Deep wounds will not be healed easily, and words may not be enough. Apology and forgiveness are made possible in the Perichoretic Space but are not inevitable. Although there is no human space that can be an entirely safe space, the Perichoretic Space is a safer space in which to practice self-giving and other-receiving. In this space, there will be judgment for oppressors, but also mercy.

21. Bosch, *Transforming Mission*, 484.
22. Parry, *Postcolonial Studies*, 19.
23. Braxton, "Paul and Racial Reconciliation," 417–18.

While the metaphor of Perichoretic Space locates the whole church within the Perichoretic Space, to engage in these Third Space encounters involves a certain degree of intentionality. Just because we sit beside someone in the pew or have an awareness of a global other does not mean we automatically engage. For example, in engaging with one another, Jesus and the Syrophoenician Woman as colonized persons intentionally enter into a Third Space encounter and participate in a discourse that defies the norms of colonizing discourse, even as the Roman Empire also hovers around that space. While power inequalities and differences remain, each is allowed to operate freely. At their point of contact arises the possibility of healing. Such a possibility occurs because God-in-Trinity inhabits Third Spaces and acts toward reconciliation and healing.

Conclusion: Locating Hope in the Midst of Empire

The Academy Award-winning film version of West Side Story colorfully and energetically brings the postcolonial struggle to life. In post-World War II Manhattan, two groups of young people are divided by race and identity. The Jets have occupied their turf for a long time. The Sharks are newcomers from Puerto Rico. The Jets jealously protect their position in the neighborhood, disputing the right of foreigners to exist within their territory. Each gang is caught up in something beyond themselves—the expectations of an older generation, a changing culture, and the increasing power and influence of the United States. The resulting disorientation of their own generation leads to tension within and between the groups. In the style of Romeo and Juliet, Tony, a Polish-American member of the Jets falls for Maria, a recent Puerto Rican immigrant whose brother is the leader of the Sharks. This romance can barely bloom in the atmosphere of hatred between the groups. Tony and Maria persist. In a violent confrontation, Tony kills Maria's brother. In the aftermath, Tony himself is shot by a member of the Jets. At the very end of the film, there is a scene that exemplifies the possibility of Third Space encounters. As Tony lies dead, Maria grieves angrily, seizing the gun and proclaiming it is hate that killed her brother and her lover. The members of both gangs look on in horror—obviously shocked at how far the violence and hatred has gone. The feud has ended. The Jets and the Sharks gather around Tony's body as Maria kisses Tony one last time. Then, young men from each side of the conflict pick up his body and carefully exit the scene of the tragedy.

Something significant happened in that space as they were gathered around the body. They recognized the fruitlessness of their conflict. Maria named out loud the hatred that brought them to that moment. The gang members were united in a common shock and common horror at what they had become. In that space of face-to-face encounter, there was a hint of mutual understanding. Reconciliation, or at least an end to an ongoing conflict, was made possible. And together, they shared the task of caring for Maria and Tony. As they left that space, carrying the body of a young man whose life was the collateral damage of a conflicted generation, they were different. Changed by the power of encounter.

For most of its existence, the Christian church has found its space of existence amid empires. With the end of Christendom, the church finds itself pushed toward the margins—a movement feared and resisted by many Christians, at least in the West. This is a time to wonder aloud if we ever belonged in the center. If the church is designed to be a reflection of a God who exists in community—shares power, suffers willingly, opens divine space to welcome creation—why should the church have preferred to imitate empire? Did the earliest churches, in their own fight for influence and survival, sell out to empire in order to receive protection and ensure their own future? Did the early church choose to mimic the actions and attitudes of its oppressors? These are not easy questions.

In a postcolonial ethos, it is time for the church to recognize its place at the margins. It is time for the church to concede its clean boundaries and be freed from the church of the past that has eschewed mixedness and ambiguity and cooperated with empire in order to gain souls. It is time to disengage, not with the world, but with the powers of empire that destroy our relationship with the world. If the church chooses to occupy the margins, then so must preaching. Postcolonial preaching is a far cry from the pulpit that stands as a symbol of authority and timelessness. Preaching that addresses postcolonial reality will be messier, less certain, more humble, more participatory.

A postcolonial homiletic, beyond participating in the transformation of discourse within the church, will also participate in a transformed praxis with regard to the mission of God's people in the world. The Perichoretic Space is a metaphor for self-giving and other-receiving, but that self-giving and other-receiving is not limited to the discursive. It is a space in which we encounter real people with real needs. Colonialism/imperialism have had negative consequences not only for human relationships, but also the material and physical well-being of millions. Preaching, as it arises in the Perichoretic Space, will lead both preacher and listeners into Third Space encounters with those who lack food, medical care, education, and other resources. As relationships are transformed, there arises the possibility that we will respond to the needs of others in a more effective and generous manner. Postcolonial preaching cannot ignore human suffering, especially as it assists listeners to share more fully in the lives of others. As churches struggle to care for poor, hungry, and sick Christians and non-Christians, a postcolonial imagination will raise questions about the manner in which aid is procured, targeted, and distributed. Brad Braxton reminds us that colonialism and slavery have left behind a flawed economic infrastructure in many formerly colonized nations: "in Ghana, a postcolonial approach to 'resurrection' that overcomes 'death' must take into account practical, tangible realities like the price of rice."[24] Preaching in the Perichoretic Space reminds us not only of the Trinity's desire for discourses of freedom, self-giving, self-differentiation, and openness, but also that those who dwell within this space will experience life in all its abundance.

In the words of Christopher Baker, who has developed a Third Space ecclesiology for postmodern urban spaces, "the Third Space is often a difficult place to be; a place where we must have the courage to face the Other in a mutual encounter, rather than hurling platitudes or insults from across the binary divide. It is, however . . . a space of renewal, excitement and new opportunity."[25] Preaching has good news for a postcolonial church that remembers and continues to endure the negative consequences of colonialism/imperialism. Recognizing that colonizing discourse inhibits Christian community, we affirm the Triune God will ultimately overcome the domination, separation, homogeneity, and fixedness of colonizing discourse. The Triune God has given us a language and an image for community that causes colonizing discourse to be "remade in other images."[26] Although the nature and possibility of the Triune God cannot ever be fully uttered,[27] preachers attempt to speak an incomplete word that points toward a promise of fulfillment. We dwell within a sacred Perichoretic Space in which healing and transformation are possible, both in this world and in the next. Here and now, we as a global church gather around tables where Christ

24. Ibid., 425.
25. Baker, *The Hybrid Church in the City*, 154.
26. Rushdie, "The Empire Writes Back with a Vengeance."
27. Brueggemann, *Theology of the Old Testament*, chapter 7.

is the host, where we see one another face to face. Around these tables, conversations begin, memories are shared, tears are shed, and there is more than enough food for all. Around such tables, we hear the Word of God promising we are not limited to what we have been. The best is yet to come.

Bibliography

Abraham, Susan. "What does Mumbai have to do with Rome? Postcolonial Perspectives on Globalization and Theology." *Theological Studies* 69 (2008) 376–93.

Alcoff, Linda Martin. "The Problem of Speaking for Others." In *Who Can Speak: Authority and Critical Identity*, edited by Judith Roof and Robyn Wiegman, 97–119. Urbana, IL: University of Illinois Press, 1995.

Allen, Ronald J. *Preaching and the Other: Studies of Postmodern Insights*. St. Louis: Chalice, 2009.

Ashcroft, Bill et al., eds. *Post-Colonial Studies: The Key Concepts*. New York: Routledge, 1998.

Baker, Christopher R. *The Hybrid Church in the City: Third Space Thinking*. Aldershot, UK: Ashgate, 2007.

Bauckham, Richard. *The Theology of Jürgen Moltmann*. Edinburgh: T. & T. Clark, 1995.

Berger, Carl. *The Writing of Canadian History: Aspects of Canadian Historical Writing in English-Speaking Canada*. 2nd ed. Toronto: Oxford University Press, 1986.

Bevans, Stephen B., and Roger P. Schroeder. *Constants in Context: A Theology of Mission for Today*. Maryknoll, NY: Orbis, 2004.

Bhabha, Homi K. "Cultures In Between." *Artforum* (September 1993) 167–214.

———. *The Location of Culture*. London: Routledge, 1994.

Boesak, Allan et al., eds. *Dreaming a Different World*. Stellenbosch: The Globalization Project, 2010.

Bonhoeffer, Dietrich. *The Cost of Discipleship*. Translated by R. H. Fuller. New York: Macmillan, 1959 [1937].

Bonzo, Matthew. *Indwelling the Forsaken Other: The Trinitarian Ethics of Jürgen Moltmann*. Eugene, OR: Pickwick, 2009.

Bosch, David. *Transforming Mission: Paradigm Shifts in Theology of Mission*. Maryknoll, NY: Orbis, 1991.

Braxton, Brad R. "Paul and Racial Reconciliation: A Postcolonial Approach to 2 Corinthians 3:12–18." In *Scripture and Traditions: Essays on Early Christianity and Judaism in Honor of Carl R. Holladay*, edited by Patrick Gray and Gail R. O'Day, 411–28. Boston: Brill, 2008.

Brueggemann, Walter. *Hopeful Imagination: Prophetic Voices in Exile*. Philadelphia: Fortress, 1986.

———. *Theology of the Old Testament: Testimony, Dispute, Advocacy*. Minneapolis: Fortress, 1997.

Campbell, Charles L. *The Word before the Powers: An Ethic of Preaching.* 1st ed. Louisville: Westminster John Knox, 2002.

Cole, Teju. "The White Saviour Industrial Complex," *The Atlantic* online, March 21, 2012.

Copeland, M. Shawn. "Body, Representation and Black Religious Discourse." In *Postcolonialism, Feminism and Religious Discourse,* edited by Laura E. Donaldson and Kwok Pui-lan, 180–98. New York: Routledge, 2002.

Crossan, John Dominic, and L. Reed. *Excavating Jesus: Beneath the Stones, Behind the Texts.* London: SPCK, 2001.

Cunningham, David S. *These Three Are One: The Practice of Trinitarian Theology.* Malden, MA: Blackwell, 1998.

Deane, Seamus. "Imperialism/Nationalism." In *Critical Terms for Literary Study,* edited by Frank Lentricchia and Thomas McLaughlin, 354–68. Chicago: University of Chicago Press, 1990.

Derrida, Jacques. "Signature Event Context." In *Margins of Philosophy,* translated by Alan Bass. Chicago: University of Chicago Press, 1982.

Donaldson, Laura E. "Postcolonialism and Bible Reading." *Semeia* 75 (1996) 1–14.

Dube, Musa. "Go Therefore and Make Disciples of all Nations (Mt. 28:19A): A Postcolonial Perspective on Biblical Criticism and Pedagogy." In *Teaching the Bible: The Discourses and Politics of Biblical Pedagogy,* edited by S. Fernando and M. A. Tolbert, 224–46. Maryknoll, NY: Orbis, 1998.

———. "Postcoloniality, Feminist Spaces and Religion." In *Postcolonialism, Feminism, and Religious Discourse,* edited by Laura E. Donaldson and Pui-lan Kwok, 100–122. New York: Routledge, 2002.

Eck, Diana L. *A New Religious America: How a "Christian Country" has Now Become the World's Most Religiously Diverse Nation.* 1st ed. San Francisco: HarperSanFransisco, 2001.

Fanon, Franz. *The Wretched of the Earth.* Translated by Constance Farrington. New York: Grove, 1963.

Farley, Edward. "Toward a New Paradigm for Preaching." In *Preaching as a Theological Task: World, Gospel, Scripture, In Honor of David Buttrick,* edited by Thomas G. Long and Edward Farley, 165–88. Louisville: Westminster John Knox, 1996.

Federov, Nicholas. *Le Christ dans la pensée Russe.* Paris: Cerf, 1970.

Fensham, Charles J. "The Glory of God Gives Life: Unmasking Subjugation for a Post-Colonial Missionary Ecclesiology in Canada." *Toronto Journal of Theology* 22/1 (2006) 55–69.

Fowl, Stephen E. *Engaging Scripture.* Oxford, UK: Blackwell, 1998.

Gandhi, Mahatma. *Collected Works, 1869–1948.* Delhi: Publications Division, Ministry of Information and Broadcasting, Government of India, 1953.

González, Catherine, and Justo González. "The Larger Context." In *Preaching as a Social Act: Theory and Practice,* edited by Art Van Seters, 29–54. Nashville: Abingdon, 1988.

González, Justo. *Liberation Preaching: The Pulpit and the Oppressed.* Nashville: Abingdon, 1980.

González, Michelle. "Who is Americana/o: Theological Anthropology, Postcoloniality and the Spanish-Speaking Americas." In *Postcolonial Theologies: Divinity and Empire,* edited by Catherine Keller et al., 58–78. St. Louis: Chalice, 2004.

Gringell, Susan. "The Absence of Seaming." In *Is Canada Postcolonial? Unsettling Canadian Literature,* edited by Laura Moss, 97–110. Waterloo, ON: Wilfrid Laurier University Press, 2003.

Hall, Douglas John. *The Cross in our Context: Jesus and the Suffering World*. Minneapolis: Fortress, 2003.

Herrick, Jennifer Anne. *Trinitarian Intelligibility: An Analysis of Contemporary Discussions and Investigation of Western Academic Trinitarian Theology of the Late Twentieth Century*. PhD Diss., University of Sydney, 2007.

Hicks, J. E. "Moral Agency at the Borders: Rereading the Story of the Syrophoenician Woman." *Word and World* 23/1 (2003) 76–84.

Horsley, Richard. *Hearing the Whole Story: The Politics of Plot in Mark's Gospel*. Louisville: Westminster John Knox, 2001.

Isasi-Diaz, Ada Maria. "A New Mestizaje/Mulatez: Reconceptualizing Difference." In *A Dream Unfinished: Theological Reflections on America from the Margins*, edited by E. S. Fernandez and F. F. Segovia, 203–19. Maryknoll, NY: Orbis, 2001.

Jefferess, David. *Postcolonial Resistance: Culture, Liberation and Transformation*. Toronto, ON: University of Toronto Press, 2008.

Jiménez, Pablo. "Toward a Postcolonial Homiletic: Justo L. González's Contribution to Hispanic Preaching." In *Hispanic Christian Thought at the Dawn of the Twenty-First Century: Apuntes in honor of Justo L. González*, edited by Alvin Padilla et al., 159–67. Nashville: Abingdon, 2005.

Keller, Catherine. "The Love of Postcolonialism: Theology in the Interstices of Empire." In *Postcolonial Theologies: Divinity and Empire*, 221–42. St. Louis: Chalice, 2004.

Keller, Catherine, et al., eds. *Postcolonial Theologies: Divinity and Empire*. St. Louis: Chalice, 2004.

Kim, Eunjoo Mary. *Preaching in an Age of Globalization*. Louisville: Westminister John Knox, 2010.

Kingsolver, Barbara. *The Poisonwood Bible*. New York: HarperFlamingo, 1998.

Kwok, Pui-lan. *Discovering the Bible in a Non-biblical World*. Maryknoll, NY: Orbis, 1995.

———. *Postcolonial Imagination and Feminist Theology*. Louisville: Westminster John Knox, 2005.

Lahiri, Jhumpa. *The Namesake*. Boston: Houghton Mifflin, 2003.

Legge, Marilyn. "Negotiating Mission: A Canadian Stance." *International Review of Mission* 95/368 (January 2004) 119–30.

Liew, Tat-Siong Benny. "Postcolonial Criticism: Echoes of a Subaltern's Contribution and Exclusion." In *Mark and Method: New Approaches in Biblical Studies*, edited by Janice Capel Anderson and Stephen D. Moore, 211–32. Minneapolis: Fortress, 2008.

Lindner, Eileen W., ed. *Yearbook of American and Canadian Churches*. Nashville: Abingdon, 2010.

Lischer, Richard. *The End of Words: The Language of Reconciliation in a Culture of Violence*. Grand Rapids: Eerdmans, 2005.

Loomba, Ania. *Colonialism/Postcolonialism: The New Cultural Idiom*. London: Routledge, 1998.

Marshall, John W. "Hybridity and Reading Romans 13." *Journal for the Study of the New Testament* 31 (2008) 157–78.

McClintock, Anne. "The Angels of Progress: Pitfalls of the Term Post-colonial." In *Colonial Discourse, Postcolonial Theory*, edited by Francis Barker et al., 253–66. New York: St. Martin's, 1994.

McDougall, Joy Ann. *Pilgrimage of Love: Moltmann on the Trinity and Christian Life*. New York: Oxford University Press, 2005.

Bibliography

McKinlay, Judith E. *Reframing Her: Biblical Women in Postcolonial Focus*. Sheffield, UK: Sheffield, 2004.

McLaren, Brian. "Post-Colonial Theology." No pages. Online: sojo.net/blogs/2010/09/15/post-colonial-theology.

McLeod, John. *Beginning Postcolonialism*. Manchester, UK: Manchester University Press, 2000.

Minh-ha, Trinh T. *Woman, Native, Other: Writing Postcoloniality and Feminism*. Bloomington, IN: University of Indiana Press, 1989.

Moltmann, Jürgen. *The Church in the Power of the Spirit: A Contribution to Messianic Ecclesiology*. Translated by Margaret Kohl. Minneapolis: Fortress, 1993.

———. *The Coming of God: Christian Eschatology*. Translated by Margaret Kohl. Minneapolis: Fortress, 1996.

———. "Communion Mediation, October 1, 1967." In *Sermons from Duke Chapel: Voices from "A Great Towering Church,"* edited by William H. Willimon, 81–85. Durham, NC: Duke University Press, 2005.

———. "Creation, Covenant and Glory." In *History and the Triune God: Contributions to Trinitarian Theology*, translated by John Bowden, 125–42. New York: Crossroad, 1992.

———. *The Crucified God: the Cross of Christ as the Foundation and Criticism of Christian Theology*. Translated by R. A. Wilson and John Bowden. Minneapolis: Fortress, 1993.

———. *Experiences in Theology: Ways and Forms of Christian Theology*. Minneapolis: Fortress, 2000.

———. *God in Creation: A New Theology of Creation and the Spirit of God*. Translated by Margaret Kohl. San Francisco: Harper and Row, 1985.

———. *Theology of Hope: On the Ground and Implications of Christian Eschatology*. Translated by James W. Leitch. New York: Harper & Row, 1967.

———. *The Trinity and the Kingdom: The Doctrine of God*. Translated by Margaret Kohl. San Francisco: Harper Collins, 1981.

Moore, Stephen D. *Empire and Apocalypse: Postcolonialism and the New Testament*. Sheffield, UK: Sheffield, 2006.

———. "Postcolonialism." In *Handbook of Postmodern Biblical Criticism*, edited by A. K. M. Adam, 55–61. St. Louis: Chalice, 2000.

Parry, Benita. *Postcolonial Studies: A Materialist Critique*. London: Routledge, 2004.

Perkinson, Jim. "A Canaanitic Word in the Logos of Christ; or, The Difference the Syro-Phoenician Woman Makes to Jesus." *Semeia* (1996).

Peters, Rebecca Todd. "The Future of Globalization: Seeking Pathways of Transformation." *Journal of the Society of Christian Ethics* 23:2 (Spring 2004) 105–33.

———. "Decolonizing our Minds: Postcolonial Perspectives on the Church." In *Women's Voices and Visions*, edited by Letty Russell et al., 93–110. Geneva, Switzerland: World Council of Churches, 2005.

Prabhu, Anjali. *Hybridity: Limits, Transformations, Prospects*. Albany, NY: SUNY Press, 2007.

Pratt, Mary Louise. *Imperial Eyes: Travel Writing and Transculturation*. New York: Routledge, 1992.

Recinos, Harold J. *Good News from the Barrio: Prophetic Witness for the Church*. Louisville: Westminster John Knox, 2006.

Reddie, Anthony. "Foreword." In *Mark and its Subalterns: A Hermeneutical Paradigm for a Postcolonial Context*, by David Joy. London: Equinox, 2008.

Richard, Pablo. "1492: The Violence of God and the Future of Christianity." In *1492–1992: The Voice of the Victims*, edited by Leonardo Boff and Virgilo Elizondo, 59–67. London: SCM, 1990.

Rose, Lucy Atkinson. *Sharing the Word: Preaching in the Roundtable Church*. Louisville: Westminster John Knox, 2007.

Rushdie, Salman. "The Empire Writes Back with a Vengeance." *The Times*, July 3, 1982.

Russell, Letty. "Cultural Hermeneutics: A Postcolonial Look at Mission." *Journal of Feminist Studies in Religion* 20 (2004) 23–40.

———. "God, Gold, Glory and Gender: A Postcolonial View of Mission." *International Review of Mission* 93 (2004) 39–49.

Said, Edward. *Culture and Imperialism*. 1st ed. New York: Knopf, 1993.

———. *Orientalism*. New York: Vintage, 2000.

———. "Yeats and Decolonization." In *Nationalism, Colonialism and Literature*, edited by Terry Eagleton et al., 69–99. Minneapolis: University of Minnesota Press, 1990.

Samuel, Simon. *A Postcolonial Reading of Mark's Story of Jesus*. London: T. & T. Clark, 2007.

Schiller, Bill. "In China, Awe and Admiration for Japan." *The Toronto Star*, March 25, 2011.

Schüssler-Fiorenza, E. *Rhetoric and Ethic: The Politics of Biblical Studies*. Minneapolis: Fortress, 1999.

Schwartz, Regina M. *The Curse of Cain: The Violent Legacy of Monotheism*. Chicago, IL: University of Chicago Press, 1997.

Segovia, F. F. "Biblical Criticism and Postcolonial Studies: Toward a Postcolonial Optic." In *The Postcolonial Bible*, edited by R.S. Sugirtharajah, 49–65. Sheffield, UK: Sheffield Academic, 1998.

Sharp, Melinda A. McGarrah. *Misunderstanding Stories: Toward a Postcolonial Pastoral Theology*. Eugene, OR: Pickwick, 2013.

Silverstein, Paul A., and Leland Conley Barrows. "Colonialism." In *Oxford Encyclopedia of the Modern World*, edited by Peter N. Stearns. No pages. Online: http://www.oxford-modernworld.com.myaccess.library.utoronto.ca/entry?entry=t254.e335-s1.

Smith, Christine M. "Preaching: Hospitality, De-Centering, Re-membering, and Right Relations." In *Purposes of Preaching*, edited by Jana Childers, 91–112. St. Louis: Chalice, 2004.

———. *Preaching Justice: Ethnic and Cultural Perspectives*. Cleveland: United Church, 1998.

Spivak, Gayatri Chakravorty. *A Critique of Postcolonial Reason: Toward a History of the Vanishing Present*. Cambridge, MA: Harvard University Press, 1999.

———. "Can the Gendered Subaltern Speak." In *Marxist Interpretations of Culture*, edited by Cary Nelson and Lawrence Grossberg. Basingstoke, UK: Macmillian, 1988.

———. "Can the Subaltern Speak?" In *Marxism and the Interpretation of Culture*, edited by Cary Nelson and Lawrence Grossberg, 271–313. Urbana, IL: University of Illinois Press, 1988.

Streets, Heather. "Gender and Empire." In *The Oxford Encyclopedia of the Modern World*, edited by Peter N. Stearns. Oxford: Oxford University Press, 2008. No pages. Online: http://www.oxford-modernworld.com.myaccess.library.utoronto.ca/entry?entry=t254.e621.

Sugirtharajah, R. S. *The Bible and the Third World: Precolonial, Colonial and Postcolonial Encounters*. New York: Cambridge University Press, 2001.

Bibliography

―――. "Complacencies and Cul-de-sacs: Christian Theologies and Colonialism." In *Postcolonial Theologies: Divinity and Empire*, edited by Catherine Keller et al., 22–38. St. Louis, MO: Chalice, 2004.

―――. "From Orientalist to Postcolonial: Notes on Reading Practices." *Asia Journal of Theology* 10 (1996) 20–27.

―――. "Imperial Critical Commentaries: Christian Discourse and Commentarial Writings in Colonial India." *Journal for the Study of the New Testament* 73 (1999) 83–112.

―――, ed. *The Postcolonial Bible*. Sheffield, UK: Sheffield Academic, 1998.

―――. *Postcolonial Criticism and Biblical Interpretation*. Oxford, UK: Oxford University Press, 2002.

―――. *Still at the Margins: Biblical Scholarship Fifteen Years after Voices from the Margins*. New York, London: T. & T. Clark, 2008.

Tanner, Kathryn. *Theories of Culture: Guides to Theological Inquiry*. Minneapolis: Fortress, 1997.

Taylor, Mark Lewis. "Spirit and Liberation: Achieving Postcolonial Theology in the United States." In *Postcolonial Theologies: Divinity and Empire*, edited by Catherine Keller et al., 39–55. St. Louis: Chalice, 2004.

Thiessen, Gerd. *The Gospels in Context: Social and Political History in the Synoptic Tradition*. Translated by Linda Maloney. Minneapolis: Fortress, 1991.

Tisdale, Leonora Tubbs. *Preaching as Local Theology and Folk Art*. Minneapolis: Fortress, 1997.

Tutu, Desmond. "The Divine Intention." In *Hope and Suffering: Sermons and Speeches*, compiled by Mothobe Mutloatse, edited by John Webster, 166–67. London: Fount, 1984.

United Church of Canada. "Living in the Midst of Empire." Report to the 39th General Council, 2006. Online: http://www.united-church.ca/economic/globalization/report.

United Nations Declaration. "World Conference against Racism, Racial Discrimination, Xenophobia and Related Intolerance." Conference, Durban: South Africa, 2001.

Verbinski, Gore, director. *The Lone Ranger*. Walt Disney Pictures, 2013.

Vergese, Abraham. *Cutting for Stone*. New York: Alfred A. Knopf, 2009.

Volf, Miroslav. *After Our Likeness: The Church as the Image of the Trinity*. Grand Rapids: Eerdmans, 1998.

―――. *Exclusion and Embrace: A Theological Exploration of Identity, Otherness and Reconciliation*. Nashville: Abingdon, 1996.

―――. "The Trinity is Our Social Program: The Doctrine of the Trinity and the Shape of Social Engagement." *Modern Theology* 14/3 (July 1998) 403–23.

Walls, Andrew. "Missionary Societies and the Fortunate Subversion of the Church." *Evangelical Quarterly* 88/2 (1988) 141–55.

Wells, Harold. *The Christic Center: Life-giving and Liberating*. Maryknoll, NY: Orbis, 2004.

Westhelle, Vitor. *After Heresy: Colonial Practices and Post-Colonial Theologies*. Eugene, OR: Wipf and Stock, 2010.

―――. *The Church Event: Call and Challenge of a Protestant Church*. Minneapolis: Fortress, 2010.

World Alliance of Reformed Churches. *Accra Confession*. Accra, Ghana, 2004. No pages. Online: http://www.warc.ch/documents/ACCRA_Pamphlet.pdf.

Wright, Jeremiah. "The Day of Jerusalem's Fall." September 16, 2001. United Trinity Church of Chicago.

————. Transcript. "Reverend Wright at the National Press Club," *New York Times*. April 28, 2008. No pages. Online: http://www.nytimes.com/2008/04/28/us/politics/28text-wright.html.

Yokota, Kariann Akemi. *Unbecoming British: How Revolutionary America Became a Postcolonial Nation*. New York, NY: Oxford, 2011.

Young, Robert J.C. *Colonial Desire: Hybridity in Theory, Culture and Race*. London, New York: Routledge, 1995.

————. *Postcolonialism: An Historical Introduction*. Oxford, UK: Blackwell, 2001.

————. *Postcolonialism: A Very Short Introduction*. Oxford, UK: Oxford University Press, 2003.

Index

Index

Index